AN EXHIBITION ORGANIZED BY THE
GEORGIA MUSEUM OF ART

Contents

Introduction

Of the many persons who have been involved in the preparation of this exhibition and catalogue, I am the only one who did not know Albert Christ-Janer personally. I came to the Georgia Museum of Art four months after his untimely death in December of 1973; we had not met elsewhere.

For this reason, it has been possible for me to approach the planning of the exhibition with an objectivity that is often difficult for a friend to assume. And I have learned that Albert Christ-Janer's friends are legion, that their memories of him are very much alive, that their recollections are colored with deep emotion, and that their individual feelings of loss remain profound. As I have read and listened, the image of an exceptional person has emerged, a man of unusual intelligence, abilities, and perspicacity. His dedication to all the arts was wholehearted, culminating in his ambitious plan for a unique national arts center, not yet realized. Throughout his life, he approached his work both as an educator and an artist in a creative and imaginative manner that has left a distinctive personal imprint on the lives of countless people and numerous institutions.

Like many Americans, particularly of his generation and earlier, Albert Christ-Janer grew up in a small-town community that was far from any major center of the arts. However, he was particularly fortunate in two respects: he received a fine musical education from his father, organist and choir director of a Lutheran church in Waterville, Minnesota; and the beginnings of his art education from Adolf Dehn, a native of Waterville where he spent his summers, who introduced the Christ-Janer boys to drawing and painting.

After graduating from Saint Olaf College where no art courses were available, Christ-Janer spent a year at the Chicago Art Institute School, followed by studies at Yale University in both the Divinity and Fine Arts Schools, receiving his Master's Degree in 1934. The broad range of his interests was reflected again in the courses he elected during a year at Harvard, 1939-40, when he studied psychology and the history of culture and education, as well as museology and art history.

Several years of teaching and administration intervened before 1948 when Christ-Janer renewed his early dedication to his own art and began to paint at every opportunity while continuing his other activities. In the 1960s, he became interested in lithography which occupied much of his attention in later years. Although his academic career included numerous and varied duties, he continued to teach since he enjoyed communicating with students and felt that his studio work and his teaching were complementary, not divisive.

Christ-Janer's early paintings were, as would be expected, strongly regionalist. During the 1950s, he moved into a calligraphic style, retaining a semblance of natural forms, but rendering these with light, deft strokes. During the 1960s, he abandoned the traditional watercolor technique and evolved a new approach, handled in a manner influenced by Abstract Expressionism, in which the inherent qualities of the medium played an important role. Of these, he wrote, "Strictly speaking, my paintings are watercolors. The papers I use may be saturated before I apply them to the board, or after; they may be thick to make an impasto or thin to effect a result like that attained by the Renaissance painter who glazed his works with layers of pigment and varnish. . . .Technically, a watercolor painting is 'one whose liquid is a water-dispersion of the binding material, which may be glue, casein, gum, etc.' . . . Recent availability of the plastic glues has increased the artist's versatility in this medium. Having experimented with the polymer glues for ten years, I simply used them as a master binding agent: pigment, paper, sands—all are mixed together, in design, and firmly held together by these wonder-working glues. This kind of painting may be the most permanent of all. . . . These works of mine, then, are not collages, which are an agglomeration of fragments and unrelated materials. Mine are personally arrived at, but technically, pure watercolors." Christ-Janer's approach to the lithographic medium was equally as innovative, as described by Clinton Adams in his essay in this catalogue.

"The earth, the sky, and the seas are my sources of information; art is my inspiration," Christ-Janer wrote at the time of his 1969 exhibition at Dartmouth College. "I am not interested in specific

PAUL WEAVER

Albert Christ-Janer

If ever a man put his heart and his soul and his beliefs and his failings and everything he had into the plain business of living, it was this cheerful, generous, well-bred and agreeable person. The sum total of his works became something more than mere "painting." It developed into a definite philosophy of life, based upon common sense and an ordinary practical sort of decency.

Albert Christ-Janer was a complicated man. I knew him for at least forty of his sixty-three years, and in many situations: as a fellow graduate student, as a novice teacher, as an administrator, as an artist, and as a friend. He brought to each area the strengths of his own complexity.

Certainly Albert was a twentieth-century man—curious, avid for knowledge, for change, and for progress. It is not easy to progress from picking beans in the bean fields of rural Minnesota to breathing wisdom into the dashingly sophisticated top levels of the art schools of Chicago, of New York, and finally of Europe.

This facility to change, to adapt to new cultural atmospheres— you can see it in his whole career. He is always devising new and more ardent ways for giving us a more and more direct picture of our friendly enemy, Nature.

Once he told me of his response to some ancient cartoons under the frescoes at Pisa which had instantly spoken to him of their time—this was the same man who thrilled to the new architecture of Mies van der Rohe, who was doing for Illinois what that other artist had done for Pisa.

Imagine a man who at the end of his daily morning jog happens into a cathedral (was it Valencia?) to rest and relax, and remembers his thrill at hearing an early-morning boy-choir rehearsing Bach— hearing it through the vast reaches of the cathedral's interior. The purity and the perfection of the tones are such as he had never heard in any calculated performance. This was the same man who recognized Roy Harris, his friend, as bringing to life many years later what he had heard at Valencia. This was the twentieth-century Albert, as I knew him: the man who could adapt from the simple

painting of the barn at Rocheport (1941) to the subtle and intricate force of the paintings and lithographs of the sixties and seventies— who could respond to the chance hearing of Bach at the old cathedral and then translate this in terms of his deep friendship with the great contemporary composer.

And then of course there was always another Albert, a sort of nineteenth-century "Renaissance Man" whose deep humanism was never so well shown as in his endless efforts to encourage his fellow artists, particularly if they were young and just starting out. I remember after he had been "best man" at my wedding and we were discussing the starting of a home, how he said to me, "Don't hang on your walls a lot of reproductions; there are thousands of originals lying around that are as good as good can be—flowers born to blush unseen?—yet the products of hundreds of fine unsung artists whose works should not be consigned to the trash heap so that they shall starve." Just as the treasure of Schubert's songs was rescued from oblivion by George Grove poking around in trunks, so many a struggling young painter owed to Albert Christ-Janer the chance to have his work hung, not in the mausoleum of an auction house, but in the light of people's homes where they would shine and be viewed with relaxed pleasure.

And in turn, Albert owed this part of his character to the deep and firm roots expressed in his deep and long-lasting friendship with the man Robert Ulich, whom he came to know and admire during his time at Harvard, until their relations became almost that of "buddies." There was this deep and firm and basic theology which ran through all of Albert's life: a driving force to help his brothers, a keen sense not only of obligation but of charity. The intense and intricate sophistication of the life he came to lead was never to deprive him of his almost innocently courageous and stout-hearted conviction of the essential goodness of humanity. No account of Albert's life could possibly be complete without great emphasis on the breadth and depth of his own personal friendships. Stanley

7

Lowell recently said to me: "We'll miss him. Every week I got a letter. For forty years." . . . . Every week! . . . For forty years, every week. . . . Deep must be the fountains from which there issues so pure and so constant a stream. And Stanley spoke movingly of how, through some mail delay, letters kept coming after Albert's actual death.

It was of course not his doing that made him the first of four brothers. But there it was, and thereafter this family of brothers was an enormous reality to him. He had the position of father-figure among them, and insisted, successfully, that they all pursue their respective educations relentlessly. This bred a solidarity of feeling which came to a head when one of them, the youngest, was so close to death the doctor came to Albert and said: "Arland's appendix has burst. This is peritonitis. He will die, unless he remains absolutely motionless for several days. If he can, I may save him. If he cannot, I cannot save him. I am unable to persuade him of this. Perhaps you can?" Albert went to his brother's bedside, and whatever passed between them made it possible for a life to be saved.

I can't help but feel that Albert's whole life exhibited this kind of harmonious and exalted mixture of—let me say—primitive ardor and civilized judgment; he was like the green tree which stands in the busy world and may be accused of uselessness while its leaves give off the very breath of life. Even though it may not acknowledge the fact, the world desperately needs pioneers like this, with their sensitive appreciations, and their struggles to put these appreciations into effect. You don't have to preach honesty to men with such a creative purpose: let a human being throw the energies of his soul into the making of something, and the instinct of workmanship will take *care* of his honesty, and his almost effort-less generosity.

I have heard his own friends sometimes taunt him because, after the critics had been good to him and his paintings became better known, he had refused to charge high prices. He said, "I *want* people to have them; that is what they are for!"

Above all, we—his personal friends—know how thoroughly he valued living in harmony with everybody. On one occasion, when some of these friends invited him to come along on a rather lengthy Great Lakes sailing trip, he asked if he might bring with him his easel and his sketch-book. I shall never forget the quiet way with which he managed to overcome the routine objections of his sailor friends by showing them that to ignore the narrow rules of sailing etiquette is not to abandon good feeling and common sense. And during the trip, they were all glad to be able to stop at one port long enough to set up an impromptu Christ-Janer exhibition at a local gallery.

Another great artist wrote his own epitaph for his own tomb in St. Paul's in London by telling those who seek his monument to look around them. There could be no better investiture for so original, so curious, so learned, and above all, so sound and hearty a man as Albert Christ-Janer.

Mentor, Ohio 1975

GIBSON A. DANES

The Dream and Metamorphosis of Vision
The Exceptional Career of Albert Christ-Janer

Prais'd be the fathomless universe,
For life and joy, and for objects and knowledge curious
Walt Whitman

As I recall, it was the summer of 1937, a very pleasant one along the shores of Lake Michigan, that I first met Albert Christ-Janer. He was serving as the visiting professor of the arts at Northwestern University, and I was in the throes of writing a master's thesis exploring the work of Toulouse-Lautrec. Our first meeting is still vivid. I was sitting in what was once the drawing room of a modest Victorian manse which housed the art department in those days. I had a stack of books on a table, but at the moment Albert came in, I still remember, I was leafing through the pages of one of Escholier's great volumes on Daumier. I have forgotten the words of exchange on our initial meeting, but I do remember we talked for a couple of hours. The conversation began with our mutual enthusiasm for Daumier and then moved around the nineteenth century with Goya, Manet, Lautrec, et al. There was that true sense of immediate rapport. We shared so many tastes, temperaments and ideas about who and what were important. There were many discussions about strategies for teaching studio work in drawing, painting, design, as well as the history of art. We also discovered how much we had in common when we would make intensive forays on the collections of paintings and drawings at the Chicago Art Institute where we had both gone to school.

Our friendship continued and matured during the next year, particularly when I was asked to join the faculty where Albert was head of the burgeoning art department at one of the remarkable educational institutions in those days, Stephens College. It was among the few experimental places and the president, James Madison Wood, had the touch and the nerve to put together an exciting faculty. For the most part, it was a youthful, ebullient group, filled with enthusiasm. William Inge and Jean Stafford taught English (it was called Communications); Kyle Morris, the painter, critic, one-time art historian, taught all sorts of things; Harry Holtzman, avant-garde abstractionist, the yet-to-be heir of the Mondrian estate, was fresh from Europe and his teaching with Hans Hofmann in New York. He offered seminars in the spring. At this moment in the late thirties, Stephens was always lively, and unpredictable, but in many ways an inspiring place. It wasn't until some time later after I left this congenial ambiance that I realized how much Albert was doing there. He couldn't have found a better place to test so many of his diverse talents. His career in education and the arts was broadly adumbrated in this stimulating, informal atmosphere which was illumined by those brilliant, highly motivated students. Without the freedom of the Stephens environment, I am now certain, his development would have been different. In the eight rigorous, demanding years there, he consciously experimented and unconsciously tested himself as an administrator of the arts, a teacher, a painter and printmaker, and a scholar-critic.

During these years in Columbia, Missouri, he had the wit and perspicacity to spend many hours with Mr. C. B. Rollins, then eighty-six, who had known George Caleb Bingham and still had in his possession a rich bundle of unpublished correspondence between his father and the artist. This initial research burgeoned and Albert scoured the state for more materials. The result was the first serious study of one of America's greatest genre painters, published in 1940. A new and imposing edition of this work has been published this year, 1975, posthumously, with a new introduction by Thomas Hart Benton.

All of his research, writing and painting were interwoven with more than a full load of studio and art history classes, but teaching was terribly important for him. He was a quiet, patient, but demanding professional instructor of drawing, composition, painting.

In this commitment to teaching, he learned to teach himself. For any number of artists, working creatively with others (and that was a prime concern at Stephens) helped greatly to sharpen both his vision and thinking. And for Albert, the subtle relationship between concept and percept, between the act and the idea, came to life for him in the teaching studio. His close association as a boy with Adolf Dehn, who was a friend and neighbor in Waterville, Minnesota, instilled in him early on a sense of expressive drawing. Albert remarked later, "I can recognize no antithesis between painting and teaching. With me, in fact, one activity fulfills the other. To paraphrase my beloved philosopher, Whitehead, this combination enables me to construct an intellectual vision of an uncommon world: it serves the zest of life by suggesting the satisfying purpose."

His future professional life was destined to be one of the most complex of almost anyone I have known. There were few who were to stretch deep moments of dedication and feel stinging frustration toward so many of the arts and with such a visionary zeal. During his multi-dimensional career, he led several lives, but all were suffused with and centered upon the arts, education, and the artist. Although he was personally committed to drawing and painting, he found a rare depth of enjoyment in music and architecture. He had a strict, not rigid, sense of Lutheran order where the fullness of sound and space could be measured with both emotion and candor.

By 1942, with the advent of World War II, the first large chapter of his professional life was fulfilled. There was a painful, traumatic interlude with the U. S. Army. He was mistakenly drafted and subject to physical discomfort that was to last for years. Possibly out of this anguish, months in a hospital, he began to search, to question at the most basic level, the problems and possibilities for the arts and the artist in our modern-democratic-capitalist-technological society. He felt deeply that the postwar years should bring fresh dividends and opportunities for the artist, composer, playwright, choreographer. Albert was both a Socratic selfless philosopher and a selfish, terribly gifted artist. He was torn, and at times he really experienced torment, but at this moment, he was truly selfless. It was a rare combination of talent, humility, and temperament.

This artistic quest was to be brought into clearer focus by his many-faceted appointment to the prestigious Cranbrook Academy in 1945. He served as Director of the Museum and Library Collections, Associate Director of the Educational Program, and Professor of Art History; but most important for his restless, questing mind was the presence of Eliel and Loja Saarinen and their brilliant son, Eero and his wife, Lily. During the interlude of the war years, Albert and Virginia spent many evenings and weekends talking and listening. Albert's youthful ambition, courage, and temerity were tempered by their wisdom.

The projected plans for the development of a National Center for the Arts were endlessly explored in this wise and relaxed company. It was here that he completed the writing for his definitive biography of Boardman Robinson, the inspiring head of the lively Colorado Springs Fine Arts Center, and he also began to gather materials for his book on the architecture of the elder Saarinen, which appeared two years later. Cranbrook was a rare oasis for gifted young people in the forties. Then, its cloistered isolation was conducive to reflection and searching analysis; in fact, the Cranbrook ambiance in those years, with its interplay of graduate study in architecture, urban planning, painting, sculpture, and the other arts of design sparked by an internationally renowned faculty, was more than a partial model for Albert's conception. He was a dreamer, but basically a realistic and practical one. He had studied enough and had traveled sufficiently to know that there was something wrong with the way the arts were dealt with, professionally, in our schools colleges and urban centers. His experience as an artist, teacher, dean, museum director, had given him a spectrum of insights, and his instincts were right.

It was an exciting and critical moment for him and within a couple of years, he had evolved a far-reaching plan for all the arts that was so logical, so brilliantly conceived, so needed, that it was all too revolutionary and ambitious for many. But innately, Albert knew that to make a great concept succeed, it had to be bold to capture the attention of potential donors. In his own words then, "The educational plan for the Arts Center is simple. The basic idea is not new. It is historically justified by many experiments from the remote and recent past, but the Arts Center plan unifies them and projects a new and total program for America. It pulls together and unites two main units: an Institute for Advanced Study and a Center for all the Visual and Performing Arts. It is to be a community of artists working together in free association. The artists and apprentices will counsel one another in the development of their works. This is the principle of creative learning, as opposed to dogmatic teaching. Such an ideal plan can be achieved by faith in the power of the assembled imagination, gathered under one roof of this center of creation and communication. In each field of the arts a distinguished artist will work with apprentices who have already achieved stature in their professions." Composer and musician; choreographer and dancer; playwright, director and actor; painters, sculptors, scholars, critics and advanced students would have their places in which to think and work. *They* would be the center. His concept began with the creativity of the individual; the bricks and mortar were secondary. He did not want marbelized monuments, but a true working center for artistic minds. The best education at the highest critical level. All of Albert's creative instincts were brought into sharp focus at Cranbrook with insight and dogged determination that made his concepts not only plausible, but in his mind, righteous. The Arts Center represented both a philosophical and practical ideal to which he would be fully committed. The arts became now publicly and personally his moral raison d'être. He was fond of saying, "Art not only has a role in education; art *is* education. And this basic fact has not been stressed frequently or vigorously enough."

Life is often filled with unexpected surprises and Albert, with his beautifully conceived plans, was ready for the unpredictable. In part, perhaps, because the audacity of his idea was only matched by its elegance, his all-embracing program caught the eye and ear of Robert M. Hutchins, the rebel president of the University of Chicago. It may seem surprising, even ironic, that Hutchins, so often stereotyped as a dogmatic neo-Thomist, would be interested in the complicated arts complex as conceived by Albert Christ-Janer almost thirty years ago. But Hutchins was a complicated, charismatic, precocious intellectual maverick. He had been just recently elevated, or had levitated himself, from the Presidency of the University to be its first Chancellor, providing him more freedom for large-scale development of the University's programs and resources. He invited Albert to become a part of his personal staff for the purpose of seeking funds for the humanities and for the projected plans for the Arts Center. Such intelligent concern and even tacit support from such a high place was encouragement that could not be ignored.

The next few years in Chicago were devoted to the sensitive social process of galvanizing community support behind the building program for the visual and performing arts center. Preliminary schematic drawings had been made and various sites were carefully studied and discussed by many influential people. By this time Albert and a small staff had garnered an impressive array of active and dedicated supporters. His energy, seriousness, and frankness captivated some of the brightest minds in America. Francis Henry Taylor, the tough-minded, scholarly director of the Metropolitan Museum wrote, "The Arts Center is the most important and most needed institution in America today." This opinion was also shared by many national leaders: Henry T. Heald, President of Illinois Institute of Technology; Fairfax Cone, President of Foote, Cone and Belding; Gaylord Donnelly, of R. P. Donnelly; Roy Harris, the composer; actors Helen Hayes and Raymond Massey, Governor Adlai Stevenson. Distinguished and numerous as were the members of this community providing national encouragement, they were men and women who were stronger in their intellectual talents than with finance. There was no lack of candid enthusiasm from the finest minds, but in almost every great project there is an inexplicable combination of timing, luck and pure chance. The first stroke of strategic misfortune was when Robert Hutchins left the University of Chicago to become the head of the Ford Foundation which then had its headquarters in Pasadena. This was a sad blow, but there had been so much widespread interest generated for the project that Albert, assisted by Richard Florsheim, with Fairfax Cone as the head of a Board of Governors and an imposing Board of Sponsors, decided to continue the development independently, with offices in downtown Chicago.

After five years of the most concentrated efforts by a large number of involved people in planning and organizing, the move was logical and plausible. A large part of the year of 1952 was spent on this second major attempt to have the first millions committed for the initial construction. This Chicago chapter of development upon which Albert and a host of others had spent almost five energetic years was to be climactically closed when Henry T. Heald, one of the early supporters of the Arts Center, left to become Chancellor of New York University where he was to be joined later by George Stoddard, then President of the University of Illinois. The sudden departure of some of the most influential people who had helped so much left a real vacuum in the windy city. Heald, however, proved to be more than a loyal friend; he was still convinced of the importance of the arts project and finally thought that in his new position in New York he could be most helpful. In October of 1952, he invited Albert to join the Chancellor's staff as Director of the Arts Center Development program. Heald was bound to see the project go ahead, and the fifties were a heady time for the arts in New York City.

By 1953 Manhattan was indeed the world center for the visual and performing arts. The gravity of creative energy had shifted rapidly from Paris to New York, hardly at the speed of the Concorde, but more like the *Ile de France*. Although New York was the most active urban arena for virtually all of the arts, and its resources were among the richest, both fiscally and in artistic responsibility, there was no true, single concentrated center for intensive professional training and performance.

The fresh presence of Henry Heald, Albert Christ-Janer, and George Stoddard at New York University awakened several artistic consciences in the city. The adventurous and boldly integrated plan for the National Arts Center was the subject of much thought and discussion by some of the most powerfully concerned citizens. There were many conferences, meetings, both formal and informal, with John D. Rockefeller III, Robert Moses, Robert Wagner, Paul Hammond, Arthur A. Houghton, Jr. et al. Arthur Judson, the manager of the Philharmonic Society became one of the most ardent supporters. The large, complicated, expensive, performing arts organizations for music, opera, dance and drama, were all seeking new or different physical facilities. These were restless years, and the mood was expansive. From the Chancellor's office in Washington Square, the reverberating effect of these many combined efforts managed to provide one of the powerful stimuli for the creation of a "Rockefeller" committee which, within a suprisingly short time would have organized the exploratory group for a "Musical Arts Center." Within a couple of years, Lincoln Center was destined to become a reality (it was called Lincoln Square, Inc., in those days) and the site for the complex was decided finally to be on the upper west side. As the planning group expanded and developed strong clusters —a real fiscal juggernaut—of officers, directors, and patrons, massive funds for the site and buildings were committed. It was a truly remarkable "west side story."

By 1955 it became clear that the plans and the dream of Albert and Henry Heald had been preempted and drastically modified. The result was both more limited in education and more expansive with marble and glass (bricks and mortar were no longer opulent enough), and the "new" center became a distortion of the original concept which had the artist and the living process of education at the heart of the plan. The profane generosity of the monumental collection of monuments reveals the truth of a comment for our time, "We are much better at building cultural complexes than we are in creating cultural complexity." I think it is a reasonable assumption that some form of the Lincoln Center complex may have come into existence because of the exigent problems with the Philharmonic and Opera, but I feel it is also true that it could not have developed so rapidly without the enormous amount of energy expended by Albert and his New York University colleagues. The interest they generated was not parochial.

After almost a decade of zealous effort for his ideas, really an ideal, there was a final ironic twist of fate when Henry Heald became the new president of the Ford Foundation, replacing Robert Hutchins. This closed an important chapter of Albert's career, that of the public visionary; but happily for him, he had the strength of his own personal, private, poetic vision which was sustained through these tumultous years. He somehow found the time and had the stamina (he was an early yoga expert) to find himself as an artist. He quietly and steadily explored many visual ideas with unusual textural, tonal and color effects. Drawing was central to his art which began to flow and coalesce into a personal style. It is not surprising that the potential of the new acrylics and polymer glues would become the basis of persistent experimentation. These New York years were to be ultimately more important to him personally than he realized then. They were blanketed by much social and administrative effort and there were moments of deep disappointment. So much genuine support and enthusiasm had been generated at the highest levels that there was cause for feeling low; however, his personal involvement with the arts and life in the Village were lively and productive. He and his wife had a lovely place for working on Perry Street, and at that time it was very close to the pulsing art world.

Despite the lack of success in establishing the National Arts Center, his imaginative administrative efforts were not a complete failure. He did manage to bestir a great many responsible and intelligent people and he generated a new sense of awareness that was not present before. One of these was Milton Eisenhower when he was President of the Pennsylvania State University. He persuaded Albert to join him in his serious attempt to create a School of the Arts on the campus, to include drama, music, and the visual arts. Albert was able to make this a reality in a relatively short time, and developed an interactive structure within which vital professional programs in all the arts could grow. With all his academic success, and the pleasant rustic air of Penn State, he was beginning to feel strongly the need for getting back to the spirited art world of New York.

At this point, I remember he called me. By that time I was at Yale and knew a number of the staff and faculty at one of the venerable professional art schools in America, the Pratt Institute. Both the Chairman of the Board and the President were most anxious for him to become Dean of the School of Art and Design, and he wondered. My advice was sincere and succinct, "You know, Albert, you had better get back to New York sooner rather than later for all that it means to you as an artist. It would also be better for Virginia." She was a brilliant librarian and archivist. However influential I may have been, by September of 1958, they were settled in Manhattan.

By the late fifties, the reputation of Pratt had begun to tarnish. It was subject to the inevitable and periodic process of academic atrophy after a long period of great success. It had reached a high point of professional training in several of the related fields of advertising, graphic, industrial design, but there ensued a lack of administrative imagination at the upper levels. Changes and fresh developments in all branches of the visual arts moved at an accelerated pace after World War II. Albert was quick to identify many of the weak areas and departments in need of both redirection and overhauling. He also recognized that Pratt had been operating as if it were at the quiet eye of a hurricane but did not realize that across the East River there were stormy revolutions underway. These winds of change are often discomforting to the misoneistic mind in either the arts or academia. It is also generally true that Pratt was not alone in being slow to perceive these creative tremors in the fine arts as well as the complex world of commercial design.

One of his first steps was to start at the beginning and he appointed a bright young designer from Yale, Lucian Krakowski (now Dean, School of Fine Arts, Washington University, St. Louis), to head up a wholly revamped Foundation Year course. And when he charged Ralph Wickiser, a pioneering artist and educator, with the mission of updating the teacher training curriculum, he also laid the basis for a new Graduate Program in painting and sculpture. For this exciting venture he not only recruited some of New York's most distinguished artists, he also found a great expanse of loft space nearby for the students to work in day and night. This combination of inspired instruction with near-ideal studio area was unmatched. Albert also sensed the need for even closer ties to Manhattan and was successful in setting up the now famous Pratt Graphics Center on lower Broadway in Greenwich Village. A second foothold in Manhattan took place in 1968 when he established the Pratt Institute Manhattan Center in an elegant midtown Park Avenue townhouse which was transformed into a variety of gallery spaces for a lively program of exhibitions.

His contribution to Pratt over a dozen years was rich, ample and varied, but unpredictably the Graphics Center was to be terribly important for his own future development as an artist. Andrew Stasik, the new director who succeeded Fritz Eichenberg, virtually thrust a stack of zinc plates into Albert's hands and told him to get to work. From that moment on, he became one of the most fervent printmakers I have ever known. The patient, imaginative suggestions of Stasik gave him that rare pleasure only to be found working closely with a dedicated printmaker who knew his craft so well. It was about this time that Albert became psychologically a part-time Dean and a full-time artist. He had finally found himself and found his way. He really knew that he was a true professional. Then he and his wife discovered a delightful secluded property in Tuxedo Park where he was able to create a fine airy working studio, the first one of his own that he had ever had.

He immersed himself in the total process of lithography. He found an endless fascination with completely unorthodox materials, techniques, methods. Printmaking, at first on zinc, with its many technical mysteries, spurred him on to a mastery of the etched, scraped, rubbed, scoured, metal plate which became the base for more untried experimentation with printing inks, tusche, gums, chemicals, and pigments. He evolved his own personal way of working which always involved a good deal of risk and uncertainty until the print was finally pulled. Implicit in his virtuoso exploitation of technique was the condensation of his brilliant conceptual imagery. Nature, in its broadest poetic sweep, is the basis for abstract forms. At times his works project an unearthly interstellar vision as if from a lunar module. He found a range of tone and texture that would accommodate the sweeping, at times dancing, play of dimly veiled light. The subtleties of medium expand into an aerial expressionism. As he said, "The earth, sky, and the sea are my sources of information; art is my inspiration."

The sixties were destined to become a significant moment of rapid invention and development for him. He virtually compressed a lifetime of work in this productive period. His works were in great demand from galleries and museums from all over the country. All sorts of important awards and prizes for his work came his way. His succession of one-man shows in New York received rave reviews from some of the most perceptive critics. "Christ-Janer's lithographs are among the most noteworthy in contemporary American art," wrote Jacob Kainen. "Obviously the work of a man of immense cultivation, they are also the work of a chance-taker with a large vision." John Canaday, "These extremely elegant and extremely deft paintings and lithographs depend on a technique of manipulating textures created. . . with a kind of chemical faultlessness." John

Gruen in *New York* magazine, "A born lyricist, he seems incapable of making a false move in works that contrive to blend vision with technique at every turn." Finally, after years devoted to so many facets of the art world, his success as an artist on his own was richly deserved.

This abundant decade which established his reputation was climaxed at the very close by a superb gesture by one of America's imaginative administrators and artists, Professor Lamar Dodd, the head of the visual arts program at the University of Georgia. He invited Albert to become the first recipient of the handsomely endowed Fuller E. Callaway Professorship in Art. He was to be provided with a studio, secretary, and a fully equipped workshop. This opportunity was too distinguished and elegant to refuse and by the fall of 1970 Albert and his wife moved into a handsome house on the Oconee River in Athens. Everything seemed to pull together. He experienced a freedom never experienced before and what Albert treasured most was that he was completely free to work and free to travel. The next summer he and his wife celebrated their thirtieth wedding anniversary in Italy and Greece. The following winter he was Artist-in-Residence at Tamarind Institute in New Mexico. Albert's work in lithography, on larger plates and with many colors, grew richer and rarer. His career has a quality of magic about it. It is amazing how all of those, often dreary, years of administration did not dampen the freshness and power of his vision. Through it all, the two most continuous filaments, really the warp and woof, of his life were his concern for helping the gifted young artist and becoming an artist himself. "As an artist," he noted, "I know I do not need to make a plea for art. There is no way to turn off the imagination, and artists will continue to work as long as any civilization remains to support them; perhaps longer."

When accidental, sudden death occurs to someone close, there is a tense unreality of disbelief. On the day he died I received a letter from him and his wife recounting the many pleasures, the rich experiences of a professional journey to the Scandinavian countries, Finland and Russia. Albert had been invited to lecture in Bergen; the next month, October, he was the guest-artist in residence at

Oslo; in Finland he was working on a new Saarinen book; in Leningrad they spent days as privileged visitors to every nook in the copious Hermitage. Their northern tour was climaxed by an invitation to serve as scholar-in-residence at the Rockefeller Foundation Center on those glorious shores of Lago di Como. They were to have one more week in Bellagio before going on to Vienna for the Christmas holidays and Albert could not help but be inspired by this, one of the most beatific of landscapes, and he still enjoyed the deep pleasure of drawing amid such bucolic splendor. He could not resist this ambiance before they returned to Georgia to begin a fresh series of works. He was really beginning to enjoy the winter and working in the south. As much as Albert loved drawing, he abhorred driving an automobile. His passion for drawing, however, was greater than his discomfort behind the wheel. There was mist in the air, dank and dusky, an atmosphere which he loved, but one which can be treacherous on those tortuous, narrow Italian roads. When the car left the road, it took the life of a very special human being.

New York, 1975

EDMUND BURKE FELDMAN

Albert Christ-Janer, Painter and Lithographer

The Swiss art historian, Heinrich Wölfflin, tried to explain why it was that Dürer, the "greatest German artist," had a longing for the South, for Italy. "Does that not imply self-renunciation?" he asked. Wölfflin answered the question by saying that "It was the apocalyptic side of Dürer that was open to the vision of Italy." Dürer's career was a continual search for ideas and images that would enable him to confirm the romantic and cataclysmic side of his nature. Of his travel and study in Italy, Wölfflin says "he took whatever he needed, without letting himself be driven from the native soil in which his imagination was rooted."[*] Surely this observation can be extended to the creative life of any artist: every environment nourishes the elements of his personality that seek visual expression. In the painting and graphic work of Albert Christ-Janer the soundness of Wölfflin's observation is confirmed: a distinctive vision of nature permeates Christ-Janer's art. No matter where he traveled, that vision made itself felt.

A native of the upper Midwest, Albert Christ-Janer was first drawn to the regionalism that was practiced by virtually every American artist of the thirties. The idea was to discover the characteristic flavor of a place, its *genius loci,* through American eyes. It was wrong to paint Pennsylvania barns, Indiana steelmills, Nebraska grain silos or Georgia cottonfields as if they had been seen through the eyes of Nicolas Poussin or Claude Lorraine. *Rocheport* (1941) is a work in which Christ-Janer paid his respects to this regionalist formula. But competent and craftsmanlike though it is, this picture seems to have been painted out of a sense of duty, the obligation felt by a young artist to carry out the prescriptions of critics and ideologues he respects. From a more personal standpoint, Christ-Janer preferred to follow a painter like Lionel Feininger, searching for the geometric order that hides behind phenomenal appearances. The regionalist formula made more sense to him when

he wrote about the great Missouri painter of historical and genre subjects—George Caleb Bingham.[**] For his own work, however, Christ-Janer sought to perfect a style that would relate him to the great nature painters of the eighteenth century. In fact, the roots of his style go back still earlier to the late medieval masters of landscape painting in Northern Europe: Cranach, Altdorfer, and Grunewald.

The Northern character of Christ-Janer's imagery found its fullest expression in the abstract language of his lithographs. As a painter, he found watercolor, tempera and gouache more congenial than oil. Watercolor especially delighted him because the whiteness of the paper encouraged the representation of his favorite qualities— light and transparency. In this medium he would apply color directly and freshly, and not as a chromatic overlay. His works in opaque media, however, sometimes lack luminosity: he seems to miss the white paper ground. As if to compensate, he builds up textures— sometimes sandy and granular, at other times coarse and corrugated, like newly erupted mountains or the eroded desert plains of Arizona and New Mexico. There is almost always a geological analogy: the tempera paintings of this period strongly resemble relief maps. They are built up layer upon layer with a dry film of color added at the end. These are somber paintings compared to the sparkling watercolors. Their seemingly spontaneous surfaces are carefully constructed; they represent Christ-Janer's endeavor to create the equivalent of the broadly painted passages which were so much admired in the Abstract Expressionist canvases of the 1950s. But his bravura display had to await his late work in lithography. This was where all those latent painterly impulses found their full expression.

In a 1972 newspaper interview, Albert Christ-Janer said: "I think that I have for the last twelve years been an astronaut, my own astronaut. People have seen the moon and astral forms in my work before the first man landed on the moon, and since then I

---

[*]Heinrich Wölfflin, *The Sense of Form in Art: A Comparative Psychological Study,* first published in 1931. Translated from the German by Alice Muehsam and Norma A. Shatan (New York: Chelsea Publishing Co., 1958), p. 17.

[**]Albert Christ-Janer, *George Caleb Bingham: Frontier Painter of Missouri* (New York: Dodd, Mead and Company, 1940).

have, of course, had many people say that I have been greatly influenced by that, and maybe I have." Taking up this same theme, Kathryn Gamble, Director of the Montclair (New Jersey) Art Museum made the following observation: "Stepping over the threshold into Christ-Janer's images is like moving effortlessly into a new but yet familiar land." Further on, she says that Christ-Janer "takes us to worlds that exist only in his inner eye." Another critic, Jacob Kainen, speaks of his basic theme as "landscape . . . conceived as a variety of elemental forces that spread, thrust, and bleed." Kainen also describes the artist as a "chancetaker." What these comments have in common is their recognition of Christ-Janer as a mystical artist who would rather paint distant worlds and inner places. His best work attempts to escape the constraints of our most familiar environments. The early attraction to the geometricism of Feininger gave way late in his career to the endeavor to represent forms without limit, spaces without boundaries. When an artist takes this path, it seems to some that he enters the world of astrophysics and extra-terrestrial travel. Picture-making ceases to be the art of representation; it becomes navigation. If Christ-Janer describes anything, it is the processes of energy exchange, of matter dissolving into light, color, and texture. At this point the imagination of the painter or printmaker is not unlike that of the medieval alchemist. The very act of seeing changes base materials into precious substances. Christ-Janer worked with some of that alchemical intensity: fastidious though his studio methods were, there was also something of wizardry about them. Collaborating closely with his printer (his assistant wizard), he experimented endlessly with the magical possibilities of positive and reversed images on photosensitive plates. He did not see technique as an end in itself so much as a means of unlocking the mystery that lies in the heart of any process of image transfer. But it was not the chemistry or physics of image-making that he cared about; it was the possibility of getting behind chemistry to some ultimate principle dealing with the transformation of matter. Albert said he was not interested in direct transcriptions of nature: realistic art bored him although he possessed conventional drawing skills. The problem with realistic representation was that it confined the artist to the surfaces of things whereas Christ-Janer wanted to penetrate to their innermost depths. While he admired Cézanne's abstract achievement, he was not especially attracted to that master's depiction of nature. Cézanne was too reasonable, which is to say too classical; Christ-Janer was convinced that reality always escapes measurement and his imagery testified to this conviction.

Lithography was for Christ-Janer a medium of technical display as well as personal expression. He handled watercolor and gouache with consummate skill, but the black, white and silvery effects of lithography evoked from him the sheer pleasure of artistic dexterity. It is obvious that he enjoyed *performing* with tusche, gum arabic; and mineral spirits on the lithographic plate. Usually, the color he added was meant to reinforce ideas already established in light and dark. Chromatic effects were almost always calculated whereas his purely lithographic imagery seemed to be a product of impulse and transient inspiration. For those who are connoisseurs of the medium, Christ-Janer's spontaneous lithographic style is a truly remarkable achievement. He was attracted to the idea that pictorial form flows from the artist's fingertips and, indeed, he liked to pour fluids onto the zinc plate, guiding their spread and spatter much as Morris Louis and Paul Jenkins orchestrated the staining of unprimed canvas with moving eddies and rivulets of wet paint.

As suggested above, Christ-Janer's approach to abstraction provides us with the best key to his overall pictorial objectives. In his mature work, he avoided geometry, measured forms, and precise boundaries, preferring to construct a world in which the classical elements—earth, air, fire and water—are dynamically intermixed. His vision of the elements is fundamentally anti-classical: they war against each other, refusing to submit to any obvious rule of mathematics or architecture—of progressive increase or decrease. It is impossible for such forms to be contained by any of the well-known schemes of modern abstraction. They merge or divide, become opaque or transparent, rise like gases or fall like rain. But they do not grow, ripen, and wither like biological forms; they do not rely on any principle of biology to explain their development. Many of the best lithographs suggest that man has not been present long enough to leave his mark. Thus we are forced to recognize Christ-Janer's images as representations of a world outside of time. Abandoning objective forms and geometric references, he pictures a teeming planet that has not yet become *cosmos;* he represents a fathomless universe before it has been fashioned according to the lineaments of human desire. He wants to show us the appearance of nature before God created the world, before there was a distinct separation between heaven and earth.

We can say of Christ-Janer's prints that the creative approach suggested the imagery. That is, the lithographic performance came first, the expressive idea followed. But the idea was not arbitrarily imposed on a random technical exercise: it is amazing how often the images allude to the same theme: the warfare between heaven and earth; the struggle of light to penetrate the barriers placed against it by landforms, sea mists, and hazy sky atmospheres. Surely there were unconscious impulses at work, deciding how to exploit the medium, selecting the themes, choosing the creative approach.

Witnessing the strategy of Christ-Janer's imagination as it recurs again and again to these immense natural dramas, one cannot help recalling one of the earliest masterpieces of Northern European nature painting. *The Battle of Issus* (1529) by Albrecht Altdorfer. Here, too, the world is seen as an arena of struggle between the luminous and the opaque. Altdorfer's landscape is more than a confrontation between the armies of Darius and Alexander; it really depicts man and nature as they clash in a final, cosmic cataclysm.

The sun blazes, the clouds swirl, the mountains are ready to explode. We see this same cosmic drama enacted—more abstractly, to be sure —in Christ-Janer's lithographs of the 1960s. Here, too, there are patches of serene color, but they are only intermittent. The pervasive theme of the lithographs is not peace but struggle—the war between light and darkness. That is what kindled his imagination, calling forth his most spontaneous and authentically felt artistic language. Altdorfer was still attached to medieval German mysticism; so he saw ogres in every tree root and mountain crag. He belonged to a tradition that was convinced of the fundamentally corrupt character of man-made forms. And while Christ-Janer was the product of a similar, fundamentally Germanic and Lutheran tradition, his lifelong artistic struggle, was to free himself from its residual pessimism: he rejoiced in the land as much as the sky. But from time to time a surviving strain of the old, medieval Manichaeism asserted itself: he would produce a lithographic statement in which the land forms are truly whited sepulchres—great structures of dead bone. Still, the optimism of the man and his work could not be dampened for long. His search for light (that was always the objective) went on to the end.

Athens, Georgia 1975

18

CLINTON ADAMS

Albert Christ-Janer at Tamarind

Let the bets that are being laid continue to tempt fortune!
André Breton, 1928

Albert had style.

In a lithographic workshop there is little room for elegance. Printers and artists are usually seen in ink-stained work clothes. Not Albert. Immaculate in a suit and vest and bow tie, an apron tied neatly around his waist, Albert brought to Tamarind a spirit as Edwardian as the touch of velvet at his collar.

He came to Albuquerque in January of 1972 in company with his wife, Miss Vee, to spend two months making lithographs. This was to be by no means his first encounter with the medium, nor his first experience in collaborative printmaking. His love affair with lithography had begun long before, in an early association with Adolf Dehn and Boardman Robinson, and had been intensified in the 1960s through active work with printers Arnold Singer, Deli Sacilotto, Michael Knigin and Jurgen Fischer.

At Tamarind he planned a series of lithographs on zinc. "Please have in stock about 30 coarse grained zinc plates as large as your pressbed can take. . . . Especially important to me is to have a sink which has a long necked faucet, so that I can put my plates under the faucet, maneuvering them to catch the flow of water. You doubtless have an adequate sink. If you have a faucet neck, say 15″ to 18″ long on a swivel, we will be okay. I must maneuver under the faucet." He also planned, he told us, to work in black and white. "I am very eager to make a depth study of black and white printing and I am frankly tired of some of the colors I have been using. . . ."

Lithography as a process depends on the fact that grease and water do not mix. The artist normally draws on the stone or plate with greasy materials—usually lithographic crayon or tusche—which will form the image. The task of the printer is then to desensitize the non-image areas and to stabilize the printing element so that an edition can be pulled in a predictable way. But as our printers were soon to learn, stability and predictability were not in Albert's mind. His working methods were designed to encourage the unexpected, the improvisation, the sudden discovery. He would have pleased Breton, for he kept open the door to chance.

His first surprise for the printers was his choice of materials. John Sommers recalls his arrival: "When he came in to begin his work we found out that he didn't plan to use any lithographic materials at all. Everything was to be drawn with stop-out materials of his own choosing—blocks of wax, chalk, white watercolor paint—almost anything that would make a mark, including cans of lacquer spray, but nothing that was greasy."

Work began. The printers quickly found out that there was no way in which they could talk Albert into using lithographic materials. They knew that because of the unconventional drawing materials his plates might respond in utterly unpredictable ways when they were processed for printing. What they didn't yet know was that nothing would please him more. Albert would eagerly stand by, watching closely as the plates were etched and rolled up. Forms would appear as if from nowhere, shapes and tones that had been invisible in the drawing, fortuitous lines and textures that were the legacy of Albert's earlier encounter with the plate beneath the flowing water. The bets that he had laid there had led to this happy fortune.

Sometimes the plate would continue to evolve even after initial proofing, even while it was being printed. Far from being bothered by this, Albert was delighted. "In one case," Sommers remembers, "I printed seventeen impressions after the *bon à tirer* had been pulled—and each of them was different. So we wound up with an extended series of proofs, not an edition." On another occasion, due to a printer's mistake, a plate changed radically. The printer feared he had a disaster on his hands. "I don't think Albert ever thought of anything as a disaster," Sommers concludes. "He just reacted to what was happening and used it constructively, as an opportunity."

19

But there are accidents and accidents.

Tamarind is located in a typical student housing area, adjacent to the University, and as are most such student areas, it is heavily populated by dogs. The Christ-Janers were staying in an apartment several blocks from the workshop. Albert later described what happened to a campus reporter. "I run every morning," he said. "On January 6—New Mexico's birthday—I was running and a dog as big as a table bit the back of my leg." But it was serious. Skin grafts were required.

Albert reacted to the accident in a characteristic manner. Just as he did in his lithographs, he used it constructively, turning to work on an unfinished manuscript for the University of Chicago Press. Simultaneously, work continued at Tamarind on plates that Albert had already completed. Sommers took proofs of the color prints to the hospital. "He had to lie on his stomach all the time. The bite was on the back of his leg and that's where the skin had been grafted, so we had to put the prints on the floor beneath his face. His head was propped up on a pillow, and when he called his nurses in to see 'these wonderful prints that this great printer had done for him' I was embarrassed by his generosity. He was a generous man, so courteous, such a grand gentleman."

When Albert returned to the workshop, still on crutches and in considerable discomfort, he abandoned color and launched immediately into a series of black and white lithographs. The air of excitement that had been lost while the printers had proofed for him in his absence was quite quickly regained. New plates followed rapidly one upon another: new gestures of line, new clouds of shimmering grays, new sparkles of black and white. Essentially, as before, the images were formed beneath the flowing water at the graining sink. But after the plates were proofed he characteristically touched them with his hand, as if to leave a personal mark, not by adding new elements but by taking out small areas, opening up white lines or scratching at tones with a wire brush or sandpaper. And, of course, given the nature of his working methods, accidents continued to happen: were *engendered,* in fact, by all that Albert did. Each accident that came along gave him ideas for new developments. The technical process became an extension of the creative one.

Then Albert and Miss Vee would take drives to Taos and Santa Fe. "Nature is the source of my information," he wrote. "Art is my inspiration." He spoke later of "the bright burst of light at the storm's edge over Albuquerque," but despite his affection for the wide skies and open vistas of New Mexico, the lithographs did not derive directly from these experiences. They were landscapes of the mind, not landscapes of time and place. Ultimately, most of his Tamarind lithographs were to be identified only by their prosaic record numbers. Even in the case of the series of small lithographs later titled *Sangre de Cristo,* the title came after the fact, as a result of one of those drives to Santa Fe, but after the images had been drawn.

It was all over too quickly. Albert invited his doctor and other friends to come in and see the prints. He spoke as always with great enthusiasm. About Tamarind as "the mecca of lithographic art," and about the fine work his printers had done for him. Then he and Miss Vee left for home.

Later, a letter came to the workshop enclosing a title page designed for the *Sangre de Cristo* series and reporting upon his plans for exhibition of the lithographs. "So thank you," he wrote. "I wish I had had more time there, but the dog did help me put out two books. . . . And so, blessings to you all."

Albuquerque, 1975

LAMAR DODD

Albert Christ-Janer, A Humanist at Georgia

When plans for the Fuller E. Callaway Professorial Chairs at the University of Georgia were being discussed, three deserving areas of excellence were named, of which Art was one. This was a signal recognition of the Department's quality—the standards it had achieved and the reputation it had gained, both in the nation and in the University at large.

But with this award came the problem of determining what qualifications we should look for in searching out the first Fuller E. Callaway Professor of Art. Not qualifications in the narrow sense of paper credentials or conventional academic success stories; rather, it was our determination to seek those personal and professional qualities which distinguish a man as a force, a power for good, an example for others. Difficult as it is to categorize the elements which constitute such a person, and to recognize them from a curriculum vitae when couched in the usual jargon, we nevertheless agreed that we wanted a person who loved to share himself with others in the teaching sense, whose intellectual curiosity as a scholar was acute, and whose creative life shaped a personal vision. This was certainly asking for a great deal—perhaps too great an order in these days of conformity and at a time when many aspects of society all too often accept mediocrity.

Albert Christ-Janer came to the campus as an examining representative of the Council of Graduate Schools in the United States when the Department's Ph.D. program was under consideration. For many of our faculty this was their first contact with him, although I had known him for many years. Albert and I were close and good friends. At that time the search for the Fuller E. Callaway Professor of Art was barely under way—and we still had very much of an open mind about the matter. Bearing this in mind I think it is a great testimonial to Albert's vital personality to recall what an effect his presence had on many of my colleagues. That intangible "power for good" to which I previously referred made itself felt in so many unpredictable ways. The natural grace and style of the man could not be avoided.

It was at this time, observing faculty response to Albert—not to mention student enthusiasm—that I began to wonder if Albert might not be the man we were looking for. And I discovered in the course of the next few days and weeks that the same thought was working in the minds of others, people whose judgment I greatly respected. But nothing was precipitated; the search continued. Only after months, when we were able to gain some objective perspective of both the nature of the job and the caliber of the people available, did the idea crystallize that we might already have found our man. It was particularly gratifying to me as Department Head that my colleagues came individually to this decision, and that Albert's ultimate appointment to the Chair was as much their wish as mine.

To condense the complex and the total of Albert Christ-Janer to a few words and phrases is impossible but, on reflection, one dominant aspect of the man comes continually to mind. It is what the Italians call "maniera," which, freely translated, means *style*—a behavior and presence beyond the commonplace—the mark of an individual dignity and graciousness, of an insight expressed in the conduct and manner of the person.

Visually he was a commanding figure; even before one talked with him, one gained the measure of his philosophy and was stimulated in the dialogue. So it is not surprising that this, together with his natural interest in people and his ease with them, made him a powerful ambassador of our Art Department and, indeed, the University as a whole. He traveled extensively, always serving our interests and singing our praises. He was the most loyal of men.

Yet in the smaller field of "home" he was equally effective. As a teacher he was available to students, able to criticize and support at the same time, helping to place both them and their works through his wide circle of contacts, and give them the hard facts about the artist's difficulties in the tough commercial market. I believe he had their complete respect. His drawing impressed them as much by its craftsmanship as by the metaphysical grandeur of his spatial visions, and his books and other writings gave them direct evidence of his intellectual acuity, the firm base of his strength and philosophy.

I think of Albert Christ-Janer as a professional man *par excellence:* that is, a fine combination of artist and teacher. His ability as an envoy representing the Department and the University was a bonus for all of us. His charm and easy friendliness made the day a little brighter.

Albert's optimistic outlook on life and his enthusiasm are beautifully expressed in a letter which I received from him within hours of the tragic news of the accident that resulted in his death. From Italy he wrote me in part:

"This is the time—when I think so much in retrospect and plan for what is coming—to tell you what your friendship means to me, Lamar. You are aware, I think, of all that you have meant to me during these past years when we worked so closely together—now at the best time of our lives I have been blessed by being in Bishop House with you. How strange and wonderful is our good fate.

"We will have an even more intimate meeting of minds when we set to work on your biography. Remembering how closely Mike [Boardman Robinson] and I worked, how well we became attuned to one another, I look forward to reviewing that rich life of yours, too. What a future we have!

"So, dear friend, we will be home soon to begin. With love, as ever,

Albert"

Athens, Georgia 1975

CATALOGUE OF
THE EXHIBITION

Catalogue of the Exhibition

PAINTINGS & DRAWINGS

Albert Christ-Janer rarely dated his works after the 1950s; the listing is chronological, using numerous approximate dates determined with the assistance of Mrs. Christ-Janer. In measurements, height precedes width.

1 *Nude,* 1930
Ink on paper, 8″ × 11″
Lent by Mrs. Albert Christ-Janer

2 *Rocheport,* 1941
Watercolor on paper, 13¾″ × 19″
Lent by Dr. & Mrs. Paul Weaver

3 *The Conversation (Business Conference),* 1944
Oil on canvas, 6¾″ × 7¾″
Lent by Dr. & Mrs. N. M. Nesset

4 *Snaggle Rock, Montana,* 1948
Watercolor on paper, 12¾″ × 17¼″
Lent by Dr. & Mrs. Paul Weaver

5 *Ellison Bay, Wisconsin,* 1950
Watercolor on paper, 7⅛″ × 9½″
Lent by Dr. & Mrs. Paul Weaver

6 *Farm at Fairbault, Minnesota,* 1950
Watercolor on paper, 8″ × 11½″
Lent by Mr. & Mrs. Burton L. Nesset

7 *Lake Bistineau, Louisiana,* 1951
Watercolor on paper, 14″ × 18″
Lent by Dr. & Mrs. Paul Weaver

8 *Shoreline of Nassau from the S. S. Nassau,* 1953
Watercolor on paper, 13½″ × 18½″
Lent by Mr. & Mrs. James W. Armsey

9 *Untitled,* 1953
Watercolor on paper, 17″ × 13½″
Lent by Mr. & Mrs. James W. Armsey

10 *Mentor Harbor Yacht Club,* 1954
Watercolor on paper, 28¼″ × 20″
Lent by Dr. & Mrs. Paul Weaver

11 *Brooklyn Navy Yard,* 1954
Watercolor on paper, 12″ × 17¼″
Lent by Mr. Branson G. Stevenson

12 *Shelter Island Bay,* 1955
Mixed media on board, 7½″ × 19¼″
Anonymous lender

13 *Spring No. 1 (New Canaan, Connecticut),* 1955
Mixed media on paper, 8″ × 5¼″
Lent by Mrs. Albert Christ-Janer

14 *Untitled (Tuxedo Park),* 1955
Watercolor on paper, 8″ × 19″
Lent by Ms. Paula Vogelsang

15 *Drawing for John Barth's "The Sot-Weed Factor,"* c. 1956-58
Pencil on paper, 12″ × 26″
Lent by Mrs. Albert Christ-Janer

16 *Seaforms E-12,* 1958
Mixed media on paper, 16⅝″ × 22⅞″
Lent by Mrs. Albert Christ-Janer

17 *No. 14,* 1959
Watercolor and collage on paper, 18⅛″ × 29¾″
Lent by The Brooklyn Museum
Dick S. Ramsay Fund

18 *Seaforms D-6,* c. 1960-70
Mixed media on board, 21⅝″ × 27″
Lent by Mrs. Albert Christ-Janer

19 *Untitled #10,* undated
Watercolor with paper collage on board, 16⅞″ × 29⅞″
Lent by Memorial Art Gallery of the University of Rochester
The Marion Stratton Gould Fund

20 *Seaforms W-99,* c. 1960-70
Mixed media on board, 11⅜″ × 19¾″
Lent by Mrs. Albert Christ-Janer

21 *Seaforms W-107,* c. 1960-70
Mixed media on board, 11½″ × 39⅜″
Lent by Mrs. Albert Christ-Janer

22 *Skyforms No. 2,* c. 1960-70
Mixed media on paper, 29½″ × 19¾″
Lent by Mrs. Albert Christ-Janer

23 *Montana Mist,* 1962
Mixed media on board, 29″ × 34″
Lent by Mr. & Mrs. Edward P. Christ-Janer

24 *B-15,* 1963
Watercolor on board, 43¼″ × 27¼″
Lent by Cranbrook Academy of Art/Museum

25 *Christmas Card Series I,* undated
Mixed media on board, 7¼″ × 20″
Lent by Dr. & Mrs. Paul Weaver

26 *Christmas Card Series II,* undated
Mixed media on board, 6½″ × 14½″
Lent by Dr. & Mrs. Paul Weaver

27 *Seaforms,* 1964
Watercolor, 26¾″ × 43″
Lent by Whitney Museum of American Art, Gift of Simon Askin

28 *Land, Sea, and Air Forms,* c. 1965-69
Mixed media on board, 23½″ × 35¼″
Lent by Mrs. Albert Christ-Janer

29 *Landforms 41,* c. 1965-69
Mixed media on board, 12″ × 33½″
Lent by Mrs. Albert Christ-Janer

30 *Skyforms W-39,* c. 1965-69
Mixed media on board, 18½″ × 21⅞″
Lent by Mrs. Albert Christ-Janer

31 *Seaforms W-49,* c. 1965-69
Mixed media on board, 14¾″ × 38½″
Lent by Mrs. Albert Christ-Janer

32 *Untitled,* c. 1965-69
Mixed media on board, 14¼″ × 39⅜″
Lent by Mrs. Albert Christ-Janer

33 *Seaforms No. 96,* 1966
Watercolor on gesso, 7¼″ × 44¼″
Lent by The Metropolitan Museum of
  Art, Gift of the Artist, 1972

34 *Untitled,* 1967
Mixed media on board, 30″ × 5½″
Lent by Ms. Paula Vogelsang

35 *Skyforms,* undated
Watercolor on paper, 10¹⁵/₁₆″ × 20″
Lent by National Collection of Fine
  Arts, Smithsonian Institution

36 *Untitled (Dartmouth #7),* undated
Mixed media, 17½″ × 35⅜″
Lent by Courtesy of the Trustees of
  Dartmouth College

37 *Untitled,* c. 1970-73
Mixed media on board, 27½″ × 43½″
Lent by Dr. & Mrs. Paul Weaver

38 *Landforms W-120,* c. 1970-73
Mixed media on paper, 7½″ × 10⅝″
Lent by Mrs. Albert Christ-Janer

39 *Seaforms G-5,* c. 1971-72
Watercolor on paper, 4¼″ × 10½″
Lent by the El Paso Museum of Art

40 *Landforms C-3* (Italian Series), 1971
Mixed media on paper, 3¾″ × 9¼″
Lent by Mrs. Albert Christ-Janer

41 *Landforms C-9* (Italian Series), 1971
Mixed media on paper, 4½″ × 13⅜″
Lent by Mrs. Albert Christ-Janer

42 *Landforms C-15* (Italian Series), 1971
Mixed media on paper, 9″ × 13″
Lent by Mrs. Albert Christ-Janer

43 *Landforms D-15* (Italian Series), 1971
Mixed media on paper, 4″ × 4″
Lent by Mrs. Albert Christ-Janer

44 *Landforms D-28* (Italian Series), 1971
Mixed media on paper, 4″ × 9¹⁵/₁₆″
Lent by Mrs. Albert Christ-Janer

45 *Landforms G-15* (Italian Series), 1971
Mixed media on paper, 4″ × 13¼″
Lent by Mrs. Albert Christ-Janer

46 *Landforms G-16* (Italian Series), 1971
Mixed media on paper, 4¼″ × 6⅛″
Lent by Mrs. Albert Christ-Janer

47 *Landforms G-17* (Italian Series), 1971
Mixed media on paper, 3¾″ × 9¼″
Lent by Mrs. Albert Christ-Janer

48 *Landforms W-152* (Italian Series),
  1971
Mixed media on paper, 4¼″ × 9⅝″
Lent by Mrs. Albert Christ-Janer

49 *Seaforms C-10 (Our Trip Along the
  Greek Isles),* 1971
Mixed media on paper,
  2¹¹/₁₆″ × 7⁹/₁₆″
Lent by Mrs. Albert Christ-Janer

50 *Seaforms G-19* (Italian Series), 1971
Mixed media on paper, 4¼″ × 13½″
Lent by Mrs. Albert Christ-Janer

51 *Seaforms W-121* (Italian Series), 1971
Mixed media on paper, 3½″ × 10½″
Lent by Mrs. Albert Christ-Janer

52 *Seaforms W-122* (Italian Series), 1971
Mixed media on paper, 5¾″ × 10½″
Lent by Mrs. Albert Christ-Janer

53 *Seaforms W-141* (Italian Series), 1971
Mixed media on paper, 5¼″ × 12″
Lent by Mrs. Albert Christ-Janer

54 *Seaforms W-142* (Italian Series), 1971
Mixed media on paper, 3⅜″ × 9⅜″
Lent by Mrs. Albert Christ-Janer

55 *Seaforms W-154* (Italian Series), 1971
Mixed media on paper, 3⁷/₁₆″ × 9¾″
Lent by Mrs. Albert Christ-Janer

56 *Seaforms W-155* (Italian Series), 1971
Mixed media on paper, 3½″ × 9¾″
Lent by Mrs. Albert Christ-Janer

57 *Seaforms W-162* (Italian Series), 1971
Mixed media on paper, 8¾″ × 11¾″
Lent by Mrs. Albert Christ-Janer

58 *Skyforms D-11* (Italian Series), 1971
Mixed media on paper, 6¼″ × 8⅜″
Lent by Mrs. Albert Christ-Janer

59 *Skyforms W-148* (Italian Series), 1971
Mixed media on paper, 3⅜″ × 9¾″
Lent by Mrs. Albert Christ-Janer

60 *Untitled,* 1970-72
Watercolor on paper, 18⅞″ × 5¾″
Lent by Mrs. Albert Christ-Janer

61 *VCJ No. 1,* 1971
Mixed media on paper, 4⅝″ × 14¼″
Lent by Mrs. Albert Christ-Janer

62 *Over the Hills and Far Away*, 1972
Mixed media on paper, 36″ × 36″
Lent by Mr. & Mrs. William E.
   Schroeder

63 *Untitled*, c. 1972
Mixed media on board,
   35½″ × 35½″
Lent by Mrs. Albert Christ-Janer

64 *Untitled*, 1972-73
Mixed media on board, 21⅝″ × 48″
Lent by Mrs. Albert Christ-Janer

65 *Skyscape* 1, 1973
Watercolor on paper, 9¾″ × 16⅝″
Lent by National Air and Space
   Museum, Smithsonian Institution

66 *Skyscape* 2, 1973
Watercolor on paper, 11⅜″ × 13½″
Lent by National Air and Space
   Museum, Smithsonian Institution

67 *Skyscape* 3, 1973
Watercolor on paper, 13¼″ × 16⅞″
Lent by National Air and Space
   Museum, Smithsonian Institution

LITHOGRAPHS

*All lithographs in the exhibition are
from the collection of Mrs. Albert
Christ-Janer with the exception of
eight from the collection of the Georgia Museum of Art which are indi-
cated. In measurements, height precedes width.*

68 *Landforms 43 (Norway)*, 1966
22⅝″ × 30½″
Edition of 30
Printer: Arnold Singer

69 *Landforms 44 (Landforms 18, Rocky
   Mountain, Western Landscape)*,
   1966
22⅜″ × 30⅛″
Edition of 30
Printer: Arnold Singer

70 *Landforms 51 (Poetic Landscape)*,
   1966
30⅛″ × 22½″
Edition of 30
Printer: Arnold Singer

71 *Landforms 83*, 1966
30⅜″ × 20¼″
Edition of 25
Printer: Arnold Singer

72 *Seaforms 42*, 1966
22⅝″ × 31⅝″
Edition of 8
Printer: Arnold Singer

73 *Landforms 78 A*, 1967
17″ × 29 9/16″
Edition of 20
Printer: Deli Sacilotto

74 *Seaforms 65 (Sacred Isle)*, 1967
30⅛″ × 22¼″
Edition of 20
Printer: Arnold Singer

75 *Seaforms 71*, 1967
10⅛″ × 28¼″
Edition of 10
Printer: Deli Sacilotto

76 *Skyforms 64 (Dawn)*, 1967
19½″ × 27⅜″
Edition: 15 large; 25 small
Printer: Michael Knigin

77 *Seaforms 75 B*, 1968
22″ × 28¼″
Edition of 15
Printer: Michael Knigin

78 *Landforms 87 B (Awakening, Sky
   Forms 23)*, 1968
22¼″ × 30″
Edition of 22
Printer: Michael Knigin

79 *Skyforms 62*, 1968
22⅛″ × 28⅝″
Edition of 15
Printer: Michael Knigin

80 *Skyforms 88*, 1968
22⅛″ × 25¼″
Edition of 20
Printer: Michael Knigin

81 *Skyforms 95*, 1968
13¹⁵⁄₁₆″ × 20″
Edition of 100
Printer: Michael Knigin

82 *Landforms 53 B*, 1969
22½″ × 30″
Edition of 30
Printer: Jurgen Fischer

83 *Landforms 54*, 1969
22⅜″ × 30⅛″
Edition of 30
Printer: Jurgen Fischer

84 *Landforms 56*, 1969
16¼″ × 26⅜″
Edition of 5
Printer: Jurgen Fischer

85 *Landforms 90*, c. 1969
22″ × 30″
Edition of 20
Printer: Michael Knigin

86 *Skyforms 57 B*, 1969
22⅜″ × 30″
Edition of 27
Printer: Jurgen Fischer
Georgia Museum of Art Collection

87 *Skyforms 57 B (Variation)*, 1969
27½″ × 22¼″
Edition unknown
Printer: Jurgen Fischer

88 *Skyforms 58 C*, 1969
22⅜″ × 30″
Edition of 12
Printer: Jurgen Fischer

89 *Skyforms 59 B*, 1969
22⅜″ × 30″
Edition of 25
Printer: Jurgen Fischer

90 *Skyforms 60 B*, 1969
22⅜″ × 21⅝″
Edition of 6
Printer: Jurgen Fischer

91 *Skyforms 60 B (Variation)*, 1969
21⅝″ × 22⅜″
Edition of 6
Printer: Jurgen Fischer

92 *Skyforms 77*, 1969
17⅞″ × 30″
Edition of 30
Printer: Jurgen Fischer

93 *Skyforms 92 A*, 1969
22″ × 19½″
Edition of 20
Printer: Michael Knigin

94 *Skyforms 92 B*, 1969
21⅞″ × 19½″
Edition of 25
Printer: Michael Knigin

95 *Far Away 76*, 1970
20⅜″ × 33¼″
Edition of 100 (IGAS)
Printer: Deli Sacilotto

96 *Landforms 97 (Distant Mountains)*,
1970
18″ × 26⅝″
Edition of 100
Printer: Unknown

97 *Skyforms 73*, 1970
24″ × 33⅞″
Edition of 100
Printer: Deli Sacilotto

98 *Skyforms 96 (Flight Path)*, c. 1970
23¾″ × 33¼″
Edition of 100
Printer: Harry Friedman

99 *Moonforms GA 15*, 1972
29⅝″ × 24⅝″
Edition of 100
Printer: Charles Massey, Jr., Bishop
House Shop, Athens, Georgia

100 *Moonforms GA 17*, 1972
29½″ × 24⅝″
Edition of 30
Printer: Charles Massey, Jr., Bishop
House Shop, Athens, Georgia

101 *Sandia Crest 101*, 1972
35″ × 22⅝″
Edition of 100
Printer: Henry Landers, The University of Georgia Printing Department
Georgia Museum of Art Collection

102 *Sandia Crest 102 A*, 1972
21¾″ × 23⅝″
Edition of 20
Printer: John Cone, The University of
Georgia Printing Department

103 *Sandia Crest 103*, 1972
35″ × 22½″
Edition of 100
Printer: John Cone, The University of
Georgia Printing Department
Georgia Museum of Art Collection

104 *Sangre de Cristo*, 1972 (T72-149—154)
7″ × 10″
Six prints from album of twelve
Edition of 10
Printer: John Sommers, Tamarind Institute, Albuquerque, New Mexico

105 *Seaforms 100*, 1972
24″ × 35″
Edition of 100 (Gift to Friends of the
Museum, Georgia Museum of Art)
Printer: Henry Landers, The University of Georgia Printing Department
Georgia Museum of Art Collection

106 *Seaforms GA 12A*, 1972
20⅝″ × 16¼″
Edition of 25
Printer: Charles Massey, Jr., Bishop
House Shop, Athens, Georgia

107 *Skyforms GA 10*, 1972
8½″ × 17″
Edition of 30
Printer: Charles Massey, Jr., Bishop
House Shop, Athens, Georgia

108 *Untitled, T72-109*, 1972
22″ × 30″
Edition of 20
Printer: John Sommers, Tamarind Institute, Albuquerque, New Mexico

109 *Untitled, T72-113*, 1972
22″ × 30″
Edition of 18
Printer: Wayne Simpkins under supervision of John Sommers, Tamarind
Institute, Albuquerque, New Mexico

110 *Untitled, T72-128,* 1972
24″ × 32″
Edition of 20
Printer: Robert Arber under supervision of John Sommers, Tamarind Institute, Albuquerque, New Mexico

111 *Untitled, T72-111A,* 1972
22″ × 30″
Edition of 20
Printer: Robert Arber under supervision of John Sommers, Tamarind Institute, Albuquerque, New Mexico

112 *Untitled, T72-602,* 1972
23″ × 24″
Edition of 10 lettered proofs and 3 trial proofs
Printer: John Sommers, Tamarind Institute, Albuquerque, New Mexico

113 *Moonforms GA 19,* 1973
27⅞″ × 16½″
Edition of 40
Printer: Charles Massey, Jr., Bishop House Shop, Athens, Georgia

114 *NASA: 10th Anniversary—63-73 II,* 1973
22⅜″ × 30″
Edition of 10
Printer: Charles Massey, Jr., Bishop House Shop, Athens, Georgia

115 *Sandia Crest 104,* 1973
30⅛″ × 20¾″
Edition of 100
Printer: John Cone, The University of Georgia Printing Department
Georgia Museum of Art Collection

116 *Sandia Crest 105,* 1973
22¾″ × 34″
Edition of 100
Printer: John Cone, The University of Georgia Printing Department
Georgia Museum of Art Collection

117 *Sandia Crest 106,* 1973
22⅝″ × 33″
Edition of 100
Printer: John Cone, The University of Georgia Printing Department
Georgia Museum of Art Collection

118 *Sandia Crest 108,* 1973
23″ × 34″
Edition of 100
Printer: John Cone, The University of Georgia Printing Department
Georgia Museum of Art Collection

Lenders to the Exhibition

Anonymous lender, Princeton, New Jersey
Mr. and Mrs. James W. Armsey, New York, New York
Mrs. Albert Christ-Janer, Athens, Georgia
Mr. and Mrs. Edward P. Christ-Janer, Great Falls, Montana
Mr. and Mrs. Burton L. Nesset, Tacoma, Washington
Dr. and Mrs. N. M. Nesset, Palatine, Illinois
Mr. and Mrs. William E. Schroeder, Sharon, Connecticut
Mr. Branson G. Stevenson, Great Falls, Montana
Ms. Paula Vogelsang, New York, New York
Dr. and Mrs. Paul Weaver, Mentor, Ohio

The Brooklyn Museum, Brooklyn, New York
Cranbrook Academy of Art/Museum, Bloomfield Hills, Michigan
El Paso Museum of Art, El Paso, Texas
Georgia Museum of Art, The University of Georgia, Athens, Georgia
Hopkins Center, Dartmouth College, Hanover, New Hampshire
Memorial Art Gallery of the University of Rochester, Rochester, New York
The Metropolitan Museum of Art, New York, New York
National Air and Space Museum, Smithsonian Institution
National Collection of Fine Arts, Smithsonian Institution
Whitney Museum of American Art, New York, New York

PAINTINGS AND DRAWINGS

2. *Rocheport*, 1941

11. *Brooklyn Navy Yard,* 1954

16. *Seaforms E-12*, 1958

17. *No. 14*, 1959

19. *Untitled #10,* undated

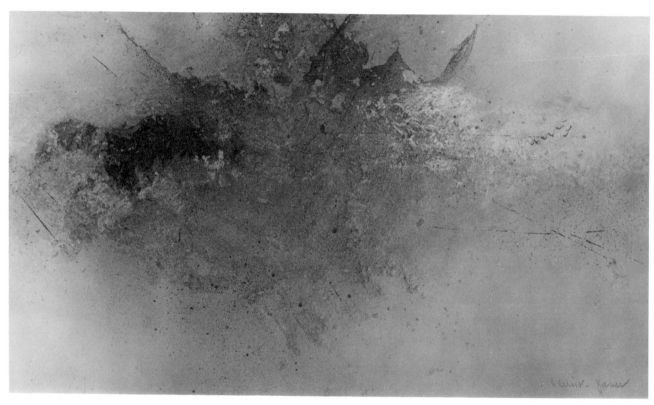

20. *Seaforms W-99*, c. 1960-70

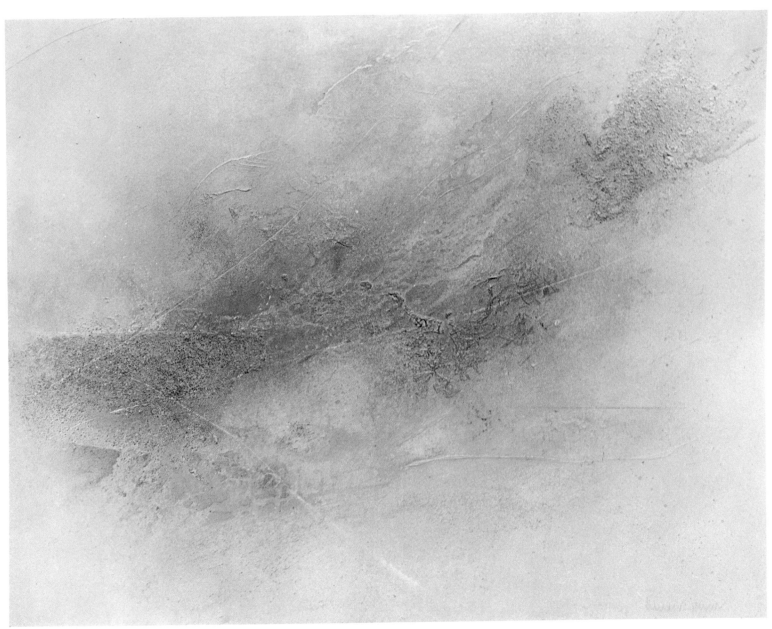

18. *Seaforms D-6*, c. 1960-70

21. *Seaforms W-107*, c. 1960-70

25. *Christmas Card Series I*, undated

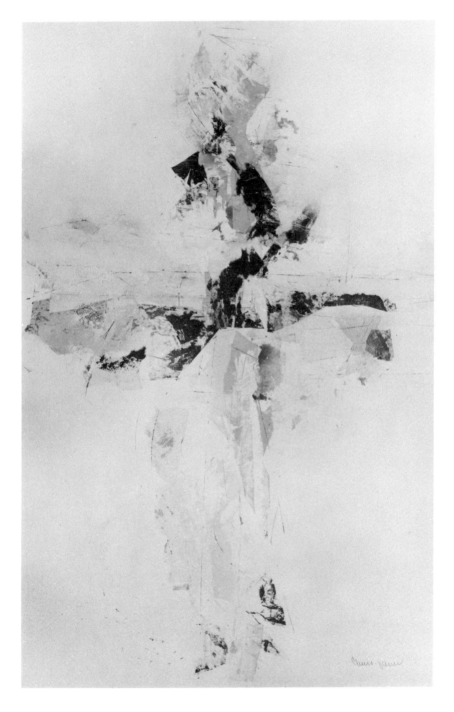

22. *Skyforms No. 2*, c. 1960-70

43

28. *Land, Sea, and Air Forms,* c. 1965-69

29. *Landforms 41*, c. 1965-69

27. *Seaforms*, 1964

46

36. *Untitled (Dartmouth #7),* undated

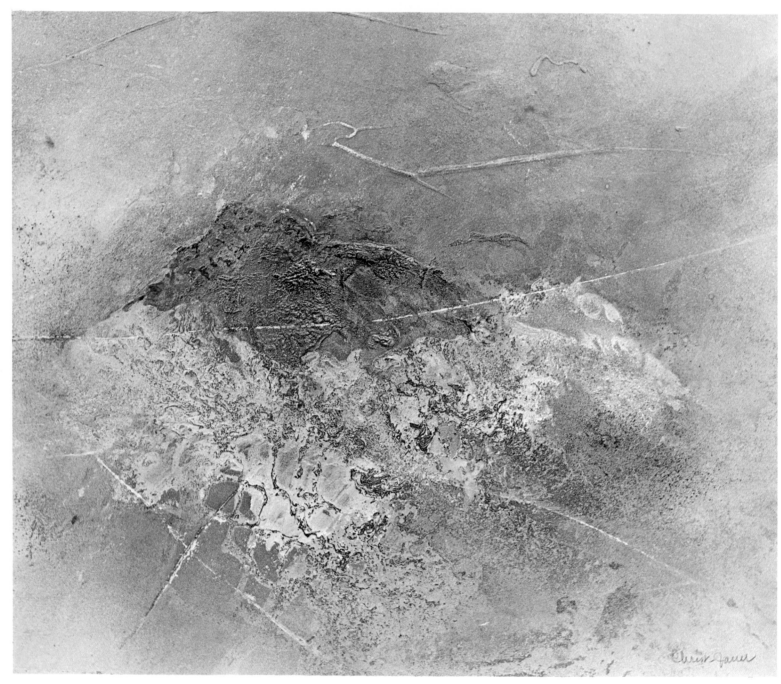

30. *Skyforms W-39*, c. 1965-69

48

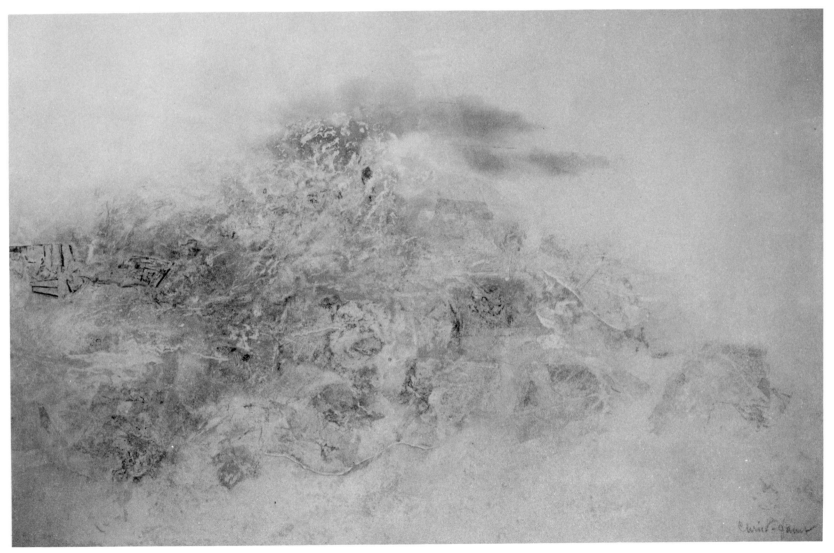

37. *Untitled*, c. 1970-73

31. *Seaforms W-49*, c. 1965-69

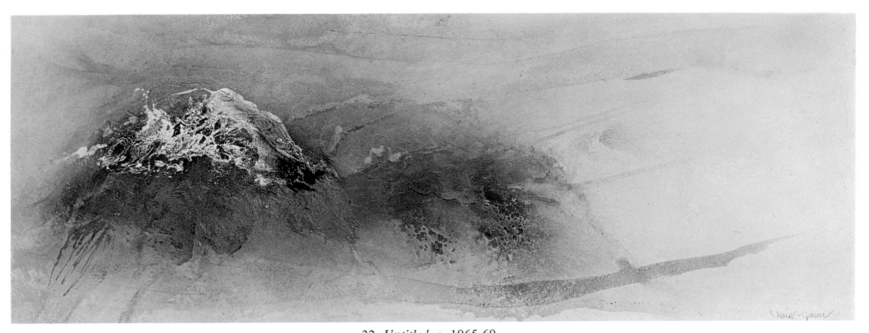

32. *Untitled,* c. 1965-69

42. *Landforms C-15* (Italian Series), 1971

63. *Untitled*, c. 1972

52. *Seaforms W-122* (Italian Series), 1971

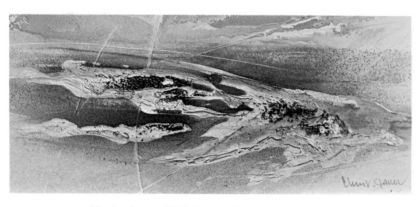

53. *Seaforms W-141* (Italian Series), 1971

64. *Untitled,* 1972-73

LITHOGRAPHS

69. *Landforms 44*, 1966

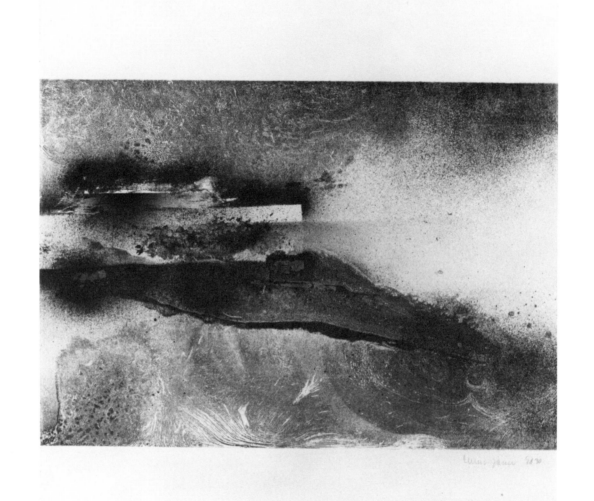

70. *Landforms 51
(Poetic Landscape),*
1966

60

71. *Landforms 83,*
1966

75. *Seaforms 71*, 1967

95. *Far Away 76*, 1970

64. *Untitled, 1972-73*

87. Skyforms 57 B (Variation), 1969

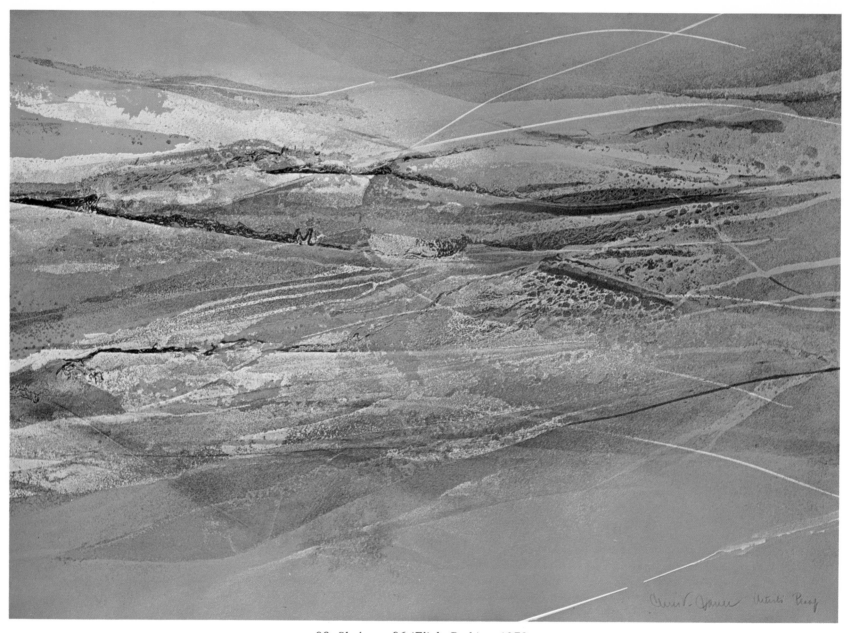

98. *Skyforms 96 (Flight Path),* c. 1970

97. *Skyforms 73*, 1970

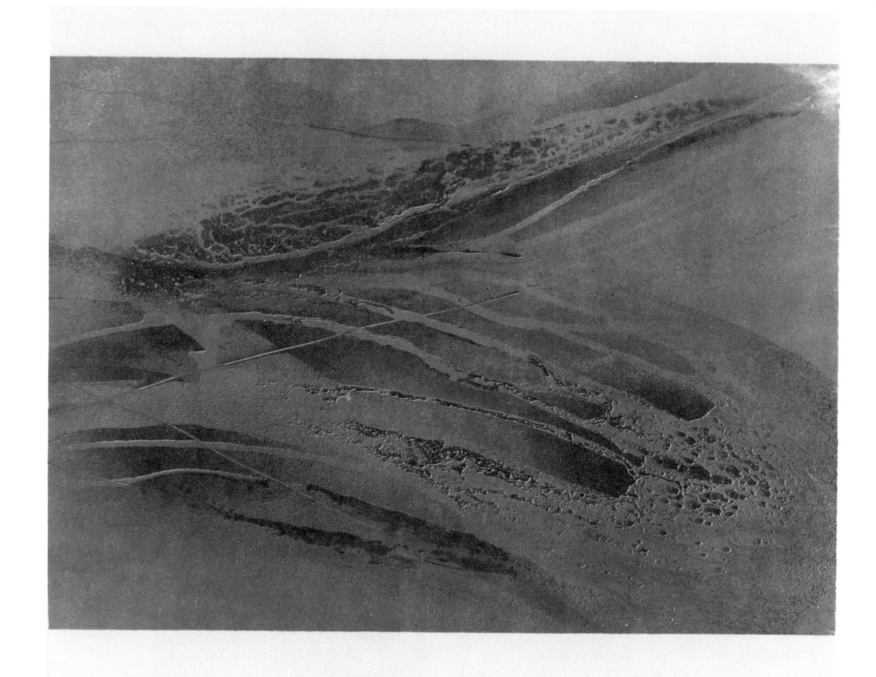

88. *Skyforms 58 C*, 1969

99.
Moonforms GA 15,
1972

102. *Sandia Crest 102 A*, 1972

108. *Untitled, T72-109, 1972*

103. *Sandia Crest 103,* 1972

105. *Seaforms 100*, 1972

109. *Untitled, T72-113, 1972*

110. *Untitled, T72-128,* 1972

113. *Moonforms GA 19,* 1973

114. *NASA: 10th Anniversary—63-73 II*, 1973

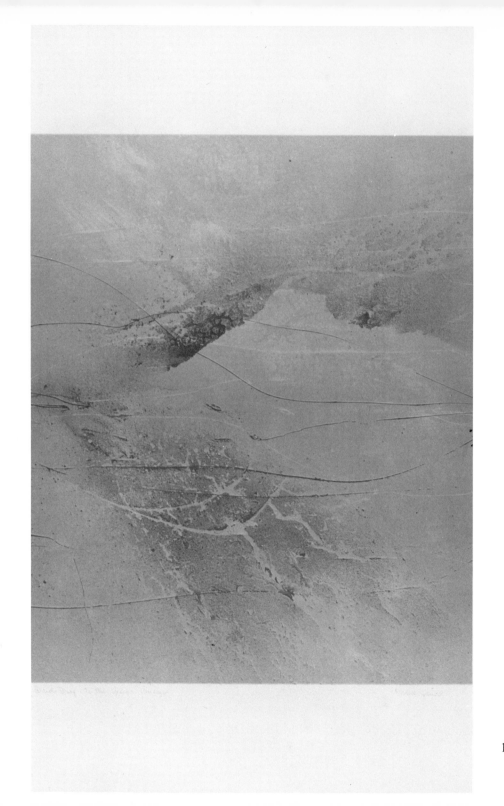

115. *Sandia Crest 104*, 1973

CHRONOLOGY

Chronology

1910 Albert William Christ-Janer was born June 13, in Appleton, Minnesota, the eldest son of William Henry and Bertha Wilhelmina Beckman Christ-Janer.

William Christ-Janer was brought to this country from Europe at the age of two years. His father had left his native Denmark, and spent several years in Hanover, Germany, before emigrating to Garland, Nebraska; in his later years he founded a Lutheran college in nearby Seward. After graduating from Addison Teachers Seminary in Addison, Illinois (now Concordia Teachers College, River Forest, Illinois), William went to Appleton, Minnesota, to become a parochial teacher at the Lutheran church school, where he was also church organist and choir director.

Bertha Beckman was the daughter of a family from Germany who also had settled in Garland, Nebraska.

1911 Albert's parents moved to Waterville, Minnesota, where his father continued his work with the Lutheran church.

1914 Edward Paul Christ-Janer was born.
Edward now lives in Great Falls, Montana, where he has an insurance business.

1915 Victor Frederick Christ-Janer was born.
A distinguished architect and educator, Victor Christ-Janer now lives in New Canaan, Connecticut.

1917 Bertha Christ-Janer had an operation which seriously affected her health and the children were sent to live with various relatives for approximately a year while she recuperated. Albert spent this time with his paternal grandfather and step-grandmother in Nebraska; he was particularly devoted to his grandfather whom he later described as a handsome man, over six feet tall, who wore a Vandyke beard.

1920s The artist Adolf Dehn, who was a native of Waterville, spent his winters in Europe and his summers in his home community. Watching him in his studio fascinated the Christ-Janer boys, especially Albert and Victor, who first worked at drawing and painting under his guidance.

1922 Arland Frederick Christ-Janer was born.
Recently appointed President of Stephens College, Columbia, Missouri, Dr. Arland Christ-Janer has been associated with college administration throughout his career.

1927 Albert Christ-Janer entered Saint Olaf College, Northfield, Minnesota.

During his college years in the great depression, Albert was employed part-time by the Associated Press as a reporter for all local sports and college events; he also served as a representative of Juster Brothers, a fine men's store in Minneapolis, that supplied him with clothes to be worn on the Saint Olaf campus as a sort of advertisement for trends in collegiate attire.

His major extracurricular activity at college was singing in the quite famous Saint Olaf choir. It continued an interest which had begun in childhood when the Christ-Janer sons sang Bach chorales every evening under the direction of their father. He did not sing after 1941 as the result of a tonsillectomy, but his interest in religious music continued; later in life, he co-authored, with Charles Hughes and Carleton Sprague Smith, a new hymnal, *American Hymns, Old and New,* not yet published. The Saint Olaf choir director was F. Melius Christianson whose sons, Olaf and Paul, were friends of Albert's; both sons became choir directors, Olaf later succeeding his father at Saint Olaf College.

Christ-Janer's college roommate was Dr. N. M. Nesset who has gained a position of eminence as a biochemist, and remained a lifelong friend.

1931 In June, Christ-Janer received his Bachelor's Degree from Saint Olaf College with a major in English (no art classes were available at that time); his most influential teachers there were George Wieda Spohn, a Shakespearean scholar, O. E. Rolvaag, author of *Giants of the Earth*, and Robert Mortvedt, later a colleague at Stephens College.

1931-32 Christ-Janer spent a school year at the School of the Art Institute of Chicago studying with Boris Anisfeldt, Francis Chapin, and Helen Gardner. Robert Bartholow Harshe, Director of the Institute, stimulated Christ-Janer's interest in writing about American art, an interest which later resulted in his books on George Caleb Bingham, Boardman Robinson, Eliel Saarinen, and other publications. Friends whom he first met during that year were Norman Rice, then a member of the Institute staff and a close associate of his later years, and Roy Rierson, a graduate of Saint Olaf, who was to become a distinguished economist in New York where they later resumed their old association.

1932 In September, Christ-Janer began a program of graduate study at Yale University, working in both the Divinity and the Fine Arts Schools. Enrollment there had been suggested to him by Donald J. Cowling, President of Carleton College, also in Northfield, who had become a close friend and advisor to the younger man during his Saint Olaf days.

In the Divinity School, the teachers he highly regarded were Roland Bainton, Robert Calhoun, and Richard Niebuhr; classmates and friends included the architect Eero Saarinen; John I. H. Baur, now Director Emeritus of the Whitney Museum of American Art; John Canaday, art critic, *The New York Times;* and Paul Weaver, his Yale roommate, who presently is President of Lake Erie College, Painesville, Ohio.

1934 In June, Christ-Janer received his Master's Degree from Yale. His thesis subject was *William Fowler Hopson of New Haven: The Last of the American Wood Engravers.*

He was appointed to the faculty at Stephens College, Columbia, Missouri, as an Instructor in the Art Department where he taught both art history and studio classes. Paul Weaver also joined the Stephens faculty as a teacher of religion and philosophy. During his years at Stephens, other members of the faculty included Maude Adams,

A visit to grandparents in Nebraska

Stephens College years

Louise Dudley, Bentley Glass, William Inge, Robert Mortvedt (formerly a teacher at Saint Olaf), Daryl Ross, Jean Stafford, Frank McMullen, and George Stoddard. Friends who were professors in the art department at the University of Missouri, also in Columbia, were Kenneth Hudson and Allen Weller.

1935-39 Grant Wood, Thomas Hart Benton and John Steuart Curry were among the lecturers he invited to the campus.

1936 In the summer, he instituted a special session for art students with a faculty which included Adolf Dehn and Victor Christ-Janer, then a graduate student at Yale, and himself; the sessions continued through the summers of 1938 and 1939.

Christ-Janer was appointed professor and head of the art department at Stephens College.

1937 Christ-Janer was appointed a professor at Northwestern University for the summer where he met and greatly enjoyed an association with Rhys Carpenter, art historian, who was teaching there at that time.

A graduate student at Northwestern, Gibson Danes, became a great friend of his during the same summer session, later introducing him to Kyle Morris; the friendship of the three of them continued throughout his life. In the fall of 1938, Christ-Janer persuaded Danes to join him in the art department at Stephens and, early in 1939, Morris also became a member of the Stephens art faculty.

1938 *Art in Child Life* by Albert Christ-Janer was published by the University of Iowa Press, Iowa City.

1939 Christ-Janer took a leave of absence from Stephens, planning to go to Europe to study at the University of London and to represent the Associated American Artists abroad, but his plans had to be cancelled shortly before sailing because of the outbreak of war in Europe that September. He enrolled at the Fogg Museum School and Harvard University where he studied museology with Paul Sachs, psychology with Gordon Allport, history of culture and education with Robert Ulich, and history of art with Arthur Pope.

1937-42 Christ-Janer presented a series of history of art lectures during the summer at Wright, Herzel and Wilson Junior Colleges, all in Chicago.

1940 *George Caleb Bingham of Missouri* by Albert Christ-Janer was published by Dodd, Mead and Company, New York.

1941 Albert Christ-Janer and Virginia Morgan Carpenter were married on May 28. Born in Dewey, Oklahoma, where her father was in the oil business, Mrs. Christ-Janer was reared in Oklahoma and Texas, and graduated from Stephens (then a junior college). She continued her studies at the University of Missouri while working part-time at Stephens, receiving her B.S. degree in Education in 1936 and her A.M. degree in 1938. During the summer of 1937, she studied at Columbia University. At the time of her marriage, she was teaching courses in World Literature at Stephens.

During their years in Columbia, the Christ-Janers lived at 1618 Anthony Avenue (May-July, 1941), 116 College Avenue (July-September, 1941), and 104 College Avenue (September, 1941—August, 1942). Mrs. Christ-Janer lived on Lawrence Place, 1942-43, while her husband was in the Army.

1942 Christ-Janer accepted the appointment as Head of the Art Department, Michigan State College (now Michigan State University). Instead of moving to Michigan, he was drafted into the Army in August in spite of a chronic back ailment that had caused his application for officer's training to be rejected. In September, he was sent to Fort Lawton near Seattle, Washington, and later transferred to Officers Candidate School in the Washington, D.C., area.

1943-45 In May of 1943, Christ-Janer received a medical discharge from the U.S. Army after a three-month stay in Walter Reed Hospital for treatment of his back. As his position at Michigan State had been held for him by President John Hannah and Dean Lloyd Emmons, he went immediately to East Lansing where he was joined in June by his wife who had taught at Stephens College during his military service; they lived at Longshadows, Okemos, Michigan (June, 1943—September,

Cranbrook, 1946

Penn State, 1956

1944), and 1132 Victor Street, East Lansing (September, 1944—May, 1945).

At Michigan State, he reorganized the department and instituted a program of visiting artists; Arnold Blanch and Boardman Robinson each taught for a quarter. During his administration, John de Martelly and Walter Abell were appointed full-time members of the department; Charles Pollock (brother of Jackson Pollock) and Jesse Garrison were also members of the art faculty at that time.

Among the visiting lecturers he invited were J. Duncan Spaeth, former professor at Princeton; Richard Hudnut, Dean of the School of Architecture at Harvard University, and Zoltan Sepeshy, Director of Cranbrook Academy of Art, who later asked Christ-Janer to join the Art Faculty there.

At the request of Ben Euwema, Head of the English Department, Mrs. Christ-Janer taught English at Michigan State during their second year in East Lansing.

1945-47 After accepting an appointment as Director of the Museum and Library, Associate Director of the Educational Program, and Professor of the History of Art at Cranbrook Academy of Art, the Christ-Janers moved to 5 Academy Road, Bloomfield Hills, Michigan, in June of 1945.

Among their friends and colleagues at Cranbrook were Eliel Saarinen, President of the Academy of Art, his wife Loja; his son Eero and wife, Lily Swann Saarinen; his daughter, "Pipsan" Saarinen Swanson and her husband, Robert; Carl and Olga Milles, Marshall Fredericks, Clifford B. West, and Maija Grotell and Marianne Stringell with whom Mrs. Christ-Janer studied weaving.

Lecturers and visitors to Cranbrook during this period included Alvar Aalto, Leonard Bernstein, Serge Chermayeff, Charles Eames, Alexander Girard, Roy and Johanna Harris, Gwen Lux, Sibyl Moholy-Nagy, Walter Quirt, Harry Weese, William R. Valentiner, William Woolfenden, and numerous visitors from abroad.

1946 *Boardman Robinson* by Albert Christ-Janer was published by the University of Chicago Press.

1947 Christ-Janer was named Director of Humanities Development at the University of Chicago by Chancellor Robert M. Hutchins, and moved to Chicago in September of 1947.

1947–52 During these years, Christ-Janer became more deeply involved with planning an arts center, an idea he had begun developing as he worked with Eliel Saarinen. He conceived the plan not only as a center for all the visual and performing arts, but also to include new and revolutionary programs for radio and television. Administration of the center would depend on a small permanent faculty and a large number of visiting artists selected from various fields of arts activity.

After Chancellor Hutchins left the University of Chicago to become President of the Ford Foundation, it became increasingly evident that such a center would not be sponsored by the University.

1948 *Eliel Saarinen* by Albert Christ-Janer was published by the University of Chicago Press.

The Christ-Janers visited his brother Edward in Great Falls, Montana, and they decided to accept Edward's invitation to spend a brief summer vacation at his cabin in the Montana mountains. During this stay, Christ-Janer began to draw and paint again, reviving his interest of earlier years. The Montana vacation marked the renewal of his commitment to his art which continued for the remainder of his life.

1950 Christ-Janer was awarded a Guggenheim Fellowship for work on a book on modern American church art and architecture.

1952 In January, Christ-Janer left the University and, with Richard Florsheim, established the Arts Center Association, Inc., with offices on Michigan Avenue, Chicago. Financially supported by Fairfax Cone and Leonard Florsheim, Sr., the organization, where Mrs. Christ-Janer worked as an unpaid assistant, continued in operation until October 1, 1952.

In Chicago, the Christ-Janers lived at 1330 East 56th Street (September, 1947—February, 1949), 1332 East 56th Street (February, 1949—June, 1950), and at The

In the studio, painting, 1941

Making a preparatory drawing for a lithograph, 1956

85

Cloisters, 5807 Dorchester (June, 1950—October, 1952).

In October, the Christ-Janers moved to New York where Henry Heald, who by then had become Chancellor of New York University, had invited him to accept the position as Director of the Arts Center Development, Office of Educational Planning. Later, at Christ-Janer's suggestion, George Stoddard was appointed Director of the Office of Educational Planning.

At that time, the University was involved in a self-study program with which Christ-Janer was actively involved. Chancellor Heald gave enthusiastic support to the plan for the Arts Center. Although many influential people in New York expressed deep interest in the concept, the plan was not financed sufficiently and was eventually abandoned after Heald resigned his position at the University to join the Ford Foundation.

In these years, Christ-Janer continued to paint and exhibit his work and he and his wife (while living at 33 Perry Street, Manhattan) were actively involved in the art world of New York.

c.1953 Christ-Janer began working with Carleton Sprague Smith on an American hymnbook. Christ-Janer had long been interested in such a project, originally planning a book of contemporary hymns, including commissioned works, to be dedicated to his father. Smith persuaded him to change the plan to include American hymns of four centuries and of all denominations, since no completely American hymnbook has been published. They received a grant from Mrs. John D. Rockefeller, Jr. (1954) to assist with this work; Charles Hughes of the music faculty of Hunter College was employed to work on the project.

1956 In February, the Christ-Janers moved to State College, Pennsylvania, where he had accepted the position of Director of the newly-established School of Fine and Applied Arts and Professor of Art at Pennsylvania State University, at the invitation of President Milton Eisenhower. Here, Christ-Janer created a school of arts—music, theatre, and the visual arts. His studio art faculty included Yar Chomicky, Stuart Frost, Hobson Pittman, George Pappas, Edwin Zoller, and George Zoretich.

With Thomas P. F. Hoving, recipient of an honorary degree, 1956

Serving on a committee to telephone Pratt Alumni

With Max Weber, recipient of an honorary degree, 1959

With Fritz Eichenberg, then head of Pratt Graphics Center

In addition to his work with art and music, Christ-Janer took an active interest in the theatre as well and was responsible for such unusual performances as the world premiere of a group of William Inge's one-act plays. Harriett Johnson, music critic on the *New York Post,* who had been commissioned to write a hymn for *American Hymns,* was also commissioned to write music for the opening of the Inge plays.

In State College, Pennsylvania, the Christ-Janers lived at 732 North Holmes Street (February-June, 1956), 519 Glenn Road (June-September, 1956), and 525 Glenn Road (September, 1956—September, 1958).

Here, again, it was Christ-Janer's ambition to create an arts center, an idea heavily endorsed by President Milton Eisenhower, who had created the School of the Arts and appointed Christ-Janer its first Director. After Eisenhower resigned to accept the Presidency of Johns Hopkins University (1957), support for the idea gradually diminished.

In June of 1956, Christ-Janer received a Doctor of Fine Arts degree from Lake Erie College, Painesville, Ohio.

1958 Richardson Pratt, Chairman of the Board of Trustees, and President Robert Oxnam of Pratt Institute, Brooklyn, invited Christ-Janer to become Dean of Pratt Institute's School of Art and Design and Professor of Art, with the idea of eventually proceeding with an arts center concept.

The Christ-Janers moved to Brooklyn where they lived at Willoughby Walk, 185 Hall Street (September, 1958—July, 1963). At the Pratt Art School, where the enrollment was approximately 2,000, Christ-Janer reorganized the curriculum and enlarged the policy of inviting well-known artists to teach for brief periods.

In November, the Christ-Janers rented a studio house on Lookout Road in Tuxedo Park, New York, where they spent weekends and holidays (November 1958—August, 1959).

Later, they bought and remodeled an old estate greenhouse on West Lake Road in Tuxedo Park which they used as home and studio from March of 1960 until their move to Georgia in August of 1970.

1960 Christ-Janer received a Guggenheim Award to assist in the publication of *Modern Church Architecture.*

1961–62 On December 28, 1961, the Christ-Janers, with their friends Dr. and Mrs. Paul Weaver, went to Europe where they visited France, Spain, Italy, and the Netherlands, returning January 30, 1962.

1962 In June and July, Christ-Janer was a guest of the government of Bonn, Germany, for visits to German museums and schools of design.

Modern Church Architecture by Albert Christ-Janer and Mary Mix Foley was published by McGraw-Hill, New York.

With the aid of Fritz Eichenberg, Christ-Janer succeeded in establishing the Pratt Graphics Center in Manhattan; when Eichenberg retired, Andrew Stasik succeeded to the directorship. Because of Stasik's persuasive suggestions, Christ-Janer started making lithographs, using zinc plates rather than stones for his work.

1963 In May, Mrs. Christ-Janer received her Master of Library Science Degree from Pratt Institute and on June 9, Christ-Janer received a Doctor of Fine Arts Degree from Saint Olaf College.

In July, the Christ-Janers moved to an apartment in Manhattan at The Buchanan, 160 East 48th Street.

1964 In January, Mrs. Christ-Janer began her work as a Librarian at the New York Public Library; in 1965 when the Research Library of the Performing Arts moved to Lincoln Center, she moved with it, later becoming Assistant Curator of the Dance Collection. She remained in this position until June, 1970.

In April, Christ-Janer visited Denmark, Norway, Finland, and Sweden to study design schools, museums, and cultural centers, accompanied by Joseph H. McCullough of the Cleveland Art Institute, John Lincoln of Rhode Island School of Design, and Norman Rice of the Carnegie Institute of Technology.

1968 Christ-Janer became the first Director of the Pratt Institute Manhattan Center, 46 Park Avenue, a branch of Pratt in Manhattan to be used for exhibitions, lectures, and meetings.

Forms by Albert Christ-Janer was published by the University of Texas, Austin.

The Christ-Janers with Joseph T. Fraser, Director of the Pennsylvania Academy of the Fine Arts, Philadelphia, and Mrs. Fraser

The Arts in Higher Education (one chapter written jointly by Albert Christ-Janer and Ralph Wickiser) was published by Jossey-Bass, Inc., San Francisco.

Christ-Janer received a grant for experimentation with lithographic processes from the American Philosophical Society of Philadelphia which was renewed in 1969. It was the first grant for studio work ever made by the Society.

1970 Christ-Janer was appointed Fuller E. Callaway Professor of Art, University of Georgia; in late August he and Mrs. Christ-Janer moved to a home they had built at River Court on the Oconee River, Athens.

1971 In the summer, the Christ-Janers went to Europe, spending June in Greece, and July and August in Italy. Their first long vacation, the Christ-Janers considered the trip a celebration of their 30th wedding anniversary.

1972 Christ-Janer was Artist-in-Residence at the Tamarind Institute, The University of New Mexico, Albuquerque, January-February.

Christ-Janer was an official NASA artist for Skylab II launch, July 25-28.

1973 In August, the Christ-Janers departed for a European trip, visiting Norway, Sweden, Denmark, Finland, Russia, and England until November 18 when they went to Bellagio, near Lake Como, Italy, where Christ-Janer was Scholar-in-Residence at the Study and Conference Center of the Rockefeller Foundation.

On December 12, Albert Christ-Janer was killed in an automobile accident at Bellagio, Italy.

1974 On January 10, a Memorial Service for Albert Christ-Janer was held at The University of Georgia Chapel.

Friends of the Georgia Museum of Art, The University of Georgia, established a Memorial Scholarship Fund, as did Pratt Institute, and Saint Olaf College.

1975 In July, *George Caleb Bingham: Frontier Painter of Missouri* was published posthumously by Harry N. Abrams. Inc., New York.

At the opening of the exhibition *Louis Bouché and Albert Christ-Janer,* January 10—February 14, 1960: with Virginia Dehn (above), with Louis Bouché and Jim Whitehead, Director of the Museum (upper right), and with the photographer Peter Pollack

At Tamarind Institute, University of New Mexico (left), with Wayne Simpkins, printer; and at The University of Georgia (right)

With Dr. and Mrs. Paul Weaver (at left) on board RMS Queen Mary, 1962

In Greece, 1971

With Wolfgang Becker, Director, Neue Galerie der Stadt Aachen (left) and Michael Rothenstein, British artist and author, 1973

With Alf R. Byercke, President of Norge-Amerika Foreningen, Oslo, before Christ-Janer's exhibition opened, 1973

THE ARTS CENTER

Albert Christ-Janer and the Arts Center Concept

One of Albert's most cherished dreams was the plan for a national arts center where professional artists and creative scholars in the fields of architecture, sculpture, painting, design, literature, music, drama, and dance would work, individually and together, and where the most talented young artists in all art media would be offered an educational program expressly devoted to their needs. The center would include, also, complete facilities for the dissemination of contemporary works of art through television and radio programming, concert presentation, exhibition, and publication.

This concept was only partially realized with the establishment of Lincoln Center for the Performing Arts in New York. Prompted by the pressing need for a permanent home for the Metropolitan Opera and the New York Philharmonic, the ultimate planners of Lincoln Center did not include the visual and literary arts; television and radio were not considered.

As far as I know, Albert coined the terms *arts center*. He started his work in Chicago using *art center,* but soon discovered that people understood the concept better if he used the plural, *arts center.*

Early in 1974, I wrote several of the men in Chicago and New York who worked with Albert on this project, requesting statements which would eventually be placed with Albert's records in the Archives of American Art.

Unfortunately, Arthur Judson, former manager of the New York Philharmonic Orchestra, director of his own agency in music, and one of the early creators of Columbia Broadcasting System, died in January, 1975, before writing anything. He was a key figure in the plans for musical development within the proposed arts center, and probably the most moving force among the professionals who influenced the building of Lincoln Center which borrowed only part of Albert's concept.

When I received Paul Hammond's statement, I learned from the accompanying letter that he had dictated it to his wife, Susan, because he is bedridden with arthritis. Two great supporters of the arts center idea have been too ill to reply to me: Fairfax Cone, partner in Foote, Cone, and Belding and former chairman of the Board of Trustees of the University of Chicago; and Lawrence A. Kimpton, former Chancellor of that institution.

Richard Florsheim, as his statement reveals, continues to believe Albert's original plan will yet be realized.

Henry Heald wrote to me from his retirement home in Florida. He died there on November 23, 1975.

I am most appreciative of these kind responses to my requests.

Virginia Christ-Janer

Athens, Georgia 1976

Paul Hammond, the financier who assembled land for the United Nations site in New York, never gave up on his idea that the Arts Center should be built on the East Side of Manhattan.

There is no doubt that the original thought of an Arts Center in this country was conceived and nurtured, not in New York, but in Chicago. During the late 1940s and early 1950s, Albert Christ-Janer and Henry Heald (later to become Chancellor of New York University) devoted their talents and energies toward building one there. They had enlisted the aid of several leaders in Chicago, among them Marshall Field, Edward L. Ryerson, Adlai Stevenson, Fairfax Cone.

Shortly after they came to New York, Albert introduced me to Henry Heald, and during our subsequent association, we formed a warm attachment to one another. They were seeking help in locating the perfect site for an Art Center. The creation of such a center had been Albert's lifelong dream. It would include art, music, drama, choreography and letters, and would be housed in a complex of handsome architectural buildings.

Our search led to a beautiful midtown situation on the East River, facing the United Nations, a building that was designed by Wallace Harrison. It would have stood at the north end of the United Nations Plaza, with a magnificent southerly view. We

95

coveted it. We showed Bob Moses some rough plans that Albert put together, and he approved them and offered to help in obtaining the necessary permission to extend them over the East River Drive, to the edge of the water.

Together, we worked long and hard on this exciting project. It would have been a glorious site.

I well remember that Albert was always in the vanguard in his efforts. His youthful zeal, indefatigable dedication, and undying faith in his dream almost won the day.

Paul Hammond

New York
  Spring 1974

Albert and Henry Heald were the first to suggest an Arts Center to John D. Rockefeller III. Rather early in their attempts to develop the concept in New York (1952), they called on him and outlined the plans.

In 1947 Albert Christ-Janer came to the University of Chicago as Director of Humanities Development. Although only 37 years of age, he had already had extensive experience in art education at Stephens College, at Cranbrook Academy, and at Michigan State University where he had been Head of the Art Department. He was already known as a painter and as a scholar with several books to his credit.

Albert's experience in the whole field of the arts had led him to the conviction that America should have a great center of the performing arts—one of the highest quality—one which would combine in one appropriate setting advanced work in painting, sculpture, drama, music, the dance and creative writing, and serve as a focus for the highest training and accomplishments in these fields.

He came to the University of Chicago, I think, with the encouragement of Robert Hutchins and in hopes that the city of Chicago might with the endorsement and the moral support of the University prove hospitable to such a concept. For several years Albert worked diligently in explaining his plan to colleagues at the University and to people in the city who might be helpful in bringing it about. In 1951 he formed the Arts Center Association through which his efforts might be focused. He was successful in attracting the interest of many of Chicago's civic leaders who supported the idea of the Art Center but were not able or not prepared to undertake the financial responsibilities it entailed. It became clear after a time that Chicago, large as it was, was not ready to embrace a concept as far-reaching and forward-looking as Albert's. The resources necessary to bring it about were unlikely to become available in Chicago.

During this period I had been president of Illinois Institute of Technology and had become acquainted with Albert Christ-Janer and his plans and hopes. I was greatly impressed by his concept and his enthusiasm for it and when in 1952 I moved to New York University, it seemed to be that if such a great center of the performing arts could be created anywhere New York City was the place for it.

Consequently I invited Albert to join the staff of the office of educational planning at New York University and to explore the art center concept in New York. This office was under the direction of George Stoddard who had recently left the presidency of the University of Illinois.* Although his responsibility was to direct a self-study of the University, in which Albert participated, he too was very much interested in the arts and the possibility of an art center. (Several years later he was, at my suggestion, asked to serve on the Lincoln Center Board.)

Albert set about to explore the opportunities for the art center with zeal and enthusiasm. He elicited the support and interest of a number of community leaders with interests in the arts, including Paul Hammond, Arthur Judson, Wallace K. Harrison and many others. He gave consideration to possible sites for the proposed center and discussed this aspect with Robert Moses who was co-operative. He visited the Rockefeller Foundation and other foundations when interest was expressed but none were prepared to under-

*George Stoddard joined the staff at New York University a year after Albert. They were old friends from George's days at the University of Iowa and Albert's at Stephens College; Albert suggested his name to Henry for the appointment as Director of the Office of Educational Planning at New York University—V. C-J.

96

take a major commitment. Unfortunately, it seemed impossible to find the financial resources to bring the project, as Albert visualized it, to function.

In 1956 I left New York University to go to the Ford Foundation and Albert Christ-Janer left to head the School of Arts at Pennsylvania State University. In the years that followed, the Lincoln Center project was proposed and eventually became a reality, and a very expensive one. Lincoln Center incorporated some but not all of Albert's original concepts. Many factors entered into the creation of Lincoln Center but I think it is likely that Albert Christ-Janer, directly and indirectly, had more influence in bringing it about than has ever been recognized.

Henry Heald

Winter Park, Florida
May 31, 1974

From January until October of 1952, Richard Florsheim worked with Albert and Virginia Christ-Janer in the offices of the newly-founded Arts Center Association, Inc. on Michigan Avenue in Chicago. Since that time, he has continued his own painting, living in both Chicago and Provincetown, Massachusetts, where he has begun the Fine Arts Work Center (with Hudson Walker), incorporating some of Albert's arts center ideas.

I first met Albert Christ-Janer at Cranbrook when I was visiting an architect friend who was completing his graduate studies with the Saarinens. It was immediately after World War II. I was very much impressed with Albert, a young, gentle, deeply thoughtful man. I felt a strong bond with him for in our very first conversation we found ourselves in agreement on a broad spectrum of ideas concerning the arts. We had some dear friends in common as well, like Adolf Dehn, who played an important role in Albert's early years, as he did in mine.

When Albert went to the University of Chicago from Cranbrook, we kept meeting from time to time at various functions. My first impression grew and deepened. When we returned from Mexico in

1951, Albert suggested that I might be helpful to the newly-forming Arts Center Association and offered me a position as his assistant in that organization. It was to be on a part-time basis, as he recognized that my first commitment was to my creative work as a painter. I accepted with enthusiasm, though with some trepidation as to my ability to be truly helpful.

In all honesty I have to declare that I was the gainer in the relationship. I learned so much from Albert on a number of levels. The organizing of committees, the involving of a variety of people in a project that was new to them, the ways of approaching foundations, the courage to face refusals and start another day without being discouraged, these and many other things were a part of the growth I experienced in my close association with him.

Albert had listened to the elder Saarinen when he suggested a new kind of institution for all the arts. That dream had found willing and eager response in the mind and heart of the young Director of the Cranbrook Museum. The idea of a kind of Institute for Advanced Studies in the arts, unknown before, matured and evolved in Albert's mind and he was able to interest Robert Hutchins in these concepts. When Hutchins invited him to the University of Chicago it was to bring to reality these ideas, "of but not in" the University.

I was very much dedicated to this concept, as Albert projected it, of an institution which was to be without grades, credits, or degrees, dedicated to the intermingling of all the arts, housed in a building of distinction where masters and their assistants would work together on real creative tasks, not academically assigned projects. That masters would live and work in an environment totally dedicated to excellence, assisted by younger professionals, already active but less experienced, was a concept that excited my imagination and was exactly what was needed. That the building would house an orchestra, theatres, studios for all the visual arts, television studios to make these efforts available to the newly-developing electronic media as a part of the forming educational networks and that all this was to take place in an open and free association seemed so vital and necessary that I could hardly believe the resistance these ideas encountered. So few people with the necessary means and "clout" seemed to understand! To me it was as necessary to do this as to breathe. Why couldn't the manufacturers, the money men, believe in it too?

Now, all these years later, I believe even more strongly in the concept. I am proud that Albert's efforts were partly responsible for Lincoln Center (as Dr. Henry Heald has written) and that the Fine Arts Work Center in Provincetown was largely shaped by the concepts I learned from my work with Albert and was able to pass along to that group.

Those were hard and wonderful times. I remember going to the Foundation offices in New York and Chicago with Albert, always with high hopes, sometimes mildly successful, often crushed by the stone wall of indifference or misunderstanding. I remember one of many such visits when we thought we had made a particularly convincing presentation and the only comment was "I don't see any provision in the budget for how the ushers are to be paid."

And I remember Albert asking me to participate in a series of lectures at the University on the "Dilemma in the Arts." I had to work hard to formulate my two lectures. The kind of hard, honest thinking that he, by example, imposed on me forced me to clarify and simplify my own enthusiasms. To this day, I use the concepts that I had to form to assist him in that series of lectures.

And I remember the courage and good sense Albert maintained as it became clear that we were not going to be able to bring off the Center in Chicago. Those last weeks when there was not enough money to pay our salaries, we worked for nothing, without any complaint on his part. I confess I complained a bit. I was not as strong or serene as Albert.

I am deeply grateful to him for, despite our failure to build our dream in Chicago, I learned a great deal that I have been able to pass on to others in some measure. Nothing done with conviction is wasted. Our efforts had their impact. The fact that those ideas of twenty years ago were ahead of their time, or that their time had not yet come, is still true. The Arts Center as Albert tried to build it will be built. The idea is still as important as it ever was.

And when it is built, those of us who knew, loved and respected this extraordinary man, will give him full credit. And I can hear him say, when that time comes: "Good things take time to evolve."

Richard A. Florsheim

Chicago
March 21, 1975

98

BIBLIOGRAPHY

Selected Bibliography

WRITINGS BY ALBERT CHRIST-JANER

William Fowler Hopson of New Haven; The Last of the American Wood Engravers. Unpublished Master's thesis, Yale University, New Haven, Connecticut, 1934.

"Art In Child Life." *Child Welfare Pamphlets,* No. 71, New Series No. 1024, University of Iowa, Iowa City, Iowa, January 14, 1938.

"The Teaching of Art Appreciation in College and High School." *School and Society.* Published for the Society for the Advancement of Education, The Science Press, Lancaster, Pennsylvania and Garrison, New York. Volume 50, Number 1296, October 28, 1939, Pages 563-566.

A review of *The Integrated School Art Program* by Leon L. Winslow. "Book Reviews," *Harvard Educational Review,* Harvard University, Boston, Massachusetts, Volume X, Number 1, January, 1940, Page 135.

"Teacher, Have I Got Talent?" *American Artist.* New York, New York, February, 1940, Volume 4, Number 2, Page 31.

George Caleb Bingham of Missouri. Dodd, Mead and Company, New York, New York, 1940.

A review of *The Visual Arts in General Education,* a report from a committee chaired by Victor E. D'Amico. "Book Reviews," *Harvard Educational Review,* Harvard University, Boston, Massachusetts, Volume XI, Number 1, January, 1941, Pages 146-147.

"Accent on Art in Michigan." *Design,* Indianapolis, Indiana, October 1943, Volume 45, Number 2, Page 20.

Boardman Robinson. University of Chicago Press, Chicago, Illinois, 1946.

Eliel Saarinen. University of Chicago Press, Chicago, Illinois, 1948.

Eliel Saarinen, Kustannusosakeyhtiö Otava, Helsingissä, 1951.

The Arts Center. New York University, New York, New York. Unpublished manuscript from the collection of Mrs. Albert Christ-Janer, 1953 or 1954. Forty pages.

"George Caleb Bingham." *One Hundred Fiftieth Anniversary Exhibition,* The Pennsylvania Academy of the Fine Arts, Philadelphia, Pennsylvania, 1955, Pages 42-45.

"The Masterbuilders." *Saturday Review,* New York, New York, May 14, 1960, Volume XLIII, Number 20, Pages 42-43.

"Landscape in the Skyline." *Saturday Review,* New York, New York, November 12, 1960, Volume XLIII, Number 46, Pages 28, 29.

(With Mary Mix Foley). *Modern Church Architecture.* McGraw-Hill (Dodge Book Dept.), New York, New York, 1962.

"Building on the Wright Foundation." *Saturday Review,* New York, New York, February 2, 1963, Volume XLVI, Number 5, Pages 36-37.

"What Part Art?" *The Journal of General Education.* The Pennsylvania State University Press, University Park, Pennsylvania, Volume 18, Number 2, July, 1966, Pages 137-141.

"What's Design?" *Art League News,* The Hazelton Art League, Inc., Hazelton, Pennsylvania, September, 1966, Pages 12 and 28.

"In Defense of Personal Expression." *American Artist,* New York, New York, October, 1966, Volume 30, Number 8, Issue 298, Pages 38-39/76, 77.

(With Ralph L. Wickiser) "Higher Education and the Arts." *The Arts in Higher Education,* Editors: Lawrence E. Dennis and Renate M. Jacob. A publication of the American Association for Higher Education. Jossey-Bass Inc., Publishers, San Francisco, California, 1968, Pages 42-59.

Forms, The University of Texas, Austin, Texas, 1968.

"An Attitude Toward The Future." *Faith & Form.* Washington, D. C., Volume 2, Number 1, January, 1969, Pages 11-14.

A chapter in *Art in American Higher Institutions,* The National Art Education Association, Washington, D.C., 1970.

George Caleb Bingham: Frontier Painter of Missouri. Harry N. Abrams, Inc., New York, New York, 1975.

ARTICLES AND CRITIQUES
(Listed alphabetically by author)

H. A. (Herb Aach?). "In the Galleries." *Arts Magazine,* Toronto, Canada, February, 1968. Volume 42, Number 4, Page 61. A review of an exhibition at Pratt Institute Gallery.

D. A. (Dorothy Adlow?). "Aquarelles at Krasner." *The Christian Science Monitor,* Arts and Entertainment Page, Boston, Massachusetts, Volume 55, Number 295, November 11, 1963, Page 6.

John C. Barnes. "Christ-Janer Work is Brilliant." *Hazelton Standard-Speaker,* Hazelton, Pennsylvania, October 17, 1966.

Jacqueline Barnitz. "In the Galleries." *Arts Magazine,* New York, New York, Volume 39, Number 5, February, 1965, Page 64.

Peter Bickel. "Art: Six-man Show at Cushing; Changeover at Dallas North." *The Dallas Times Herald,* Dallas, Texas, Volume 93, Number 145, May 25, 1969, Page D-7.

Jon Borgzinner. "Watercolors/Visions from the Greenhouse." *Time,* New York, New York, December 31, 1965, Volume 86, Number 27, Page 74, 75.

Emily Brower. "Christ-Janer Exhibition Displays Fragile Beauty." *Swarthmore College Phoenix,* Swarthmore, Pennsylvania, December 19, 1967, Page number unknown.

Rosalind Browne. "Reviews and Previews." *Art News,* New York, New York, Volume 63, Number 9, January, 1965, Page 16.

Rosalind Browne. "Reviews and Previews." *Art News,* New York, New York, February, 1966, Volume 64, Number 10, Page 14. A review of exhibition at Krasner Gallery.

Rosalind Browne. "Reviews and Previews." *Art News,* New York, New York, February, 1967, Volume 65, Number 10, Page 12. A review of exhibition at Krasner Gallery.

Clyde Burnett. "Two-Phase Christ-Janer Exhibit Is Elegant." *The Atlanta Journal.* Atlanta, Georgia, January 26, 1973, Page 18-A.

John Canaday. "A History of Painting in 3 Installments." *The New York Times,* New York, New York, January 14, 1967. Reviews of New York exhibition including Albert Christ-Janer's one-man show at Krasner Gallery, Page number unknown.

John Canaday. "Art: Dubuffet's World of 'Hourloupe'." *The New York Times,* New York, New York, March 2, 1968. Reviews of New York exhibitions including Albert Christ-Janer's one-man show at Krasner Gallery, Page 21.

Frank Caspers. "Bingham of Missouri." *The Art Digest,* Hopewell, New Jersey, May 1, 1940, Volume XIV, Number 15, Page 31.

Frank Caspers. *"George Caleb Bingham, Painter of a Midwest Frontier." The New York Times,* New York, New York Book Review, May 12, 1940, Volume LXXXLX, Number 30,059, Section 6, Page 4. A review of *George Caleb Bingham.*

Yar G. Chomicky. *Watercolor Painting.* Prentice-Hall, Inc., Englewood, New Jersey, 1968, Page 117, Illustration in color.

Marianne Cole. "Polymer Paintings May Last Forever." *Brooklyn World-Telegram,* Brooklyn, New York, December 29, 1965, Page B-1.

Marianne Cole. "Museum Exhibits Paintings by Pratt's Dean, Christ-Janer." *New York World-Telegram and The Sun,* New York, New York, December 29, 1965, Page number unknown.

Thomas Craven. "Great Artist, Man of Integrity." *The New York Herald Tribune,* New York, New York, Book Review, December 1, 1946, Volume CVI, Number 36,540, Section VII, Page 4. A review of *Boardman Robinson.*

Howard Devree. *"Many Sided Artist." The New York Times,* New York, New York, Book Review, December 29, 1946, Volume XCVI, Number 32,481, Section 7, Page 9. A review of *Boardman Robinson.*

Victoria Donohoe. "Art." *Philadelphia Inquirer,* Philadelphia, Pennsylvania, Volume 290, Number 32, February 1, 1974, Page 2-D.

Eugene M. Ettenberg. "The Pratt Graphic Art Center." *American Artist,* New York, New York, May, 1964, Volume 28, Number 5, Issue 275, Pages 34-38/62, 63, 64, 65.

Gregg Fales. "Christ-Janer Prints Masterful." *The Morning Call,* Allentown, Pennsylvania. Volume 26,226, May 10, 1971, Page 4.

Benjamin Forgrey. "Triumphs of Craft." *The Evening Star-Daily News,* Washington, D. C., June 12, 1973, Page number unknown.

John Forwalter. "Into the Work." *The Chicago Herald,* Chicago, Illinois, June 6, 1973, Page 12.

John Gardner. "Acrylics, Lithographs Distinguish Christ-Janer." *The Dartmouth,* Dartmouth College, Hanover, New Hampshire. Volume CXXVIII, Number 81, February 14, 1969, Page 3.

Emily Genauer. "In the Art Galleries." Reviews of New York exhibition including Albert Christ-Janer's one-man show at Krasner Gallery, *New York Herald Tribune,* New York, New York, December 19, 1964, Page number unknown.

Emily Genauer. "Art Tour; Critical Guide to the Galleries." *New York Herald Tribune,* New York, New York, Volume CXXV, Number 43,377, January 8, 1966, Page 9.

Jane Gollin. "Pratt Institute Expands." *Art Voices,* New York, New York, Fall, 1965, Pages 108-109.

Jane Gollin. "Reviews and Previews." *Art News,* New York, New York, March, 1968, Volume 67, Number 1, Page 12. A review of Krasner Gallery exhibition.

Percival Goodman. "The Inner Spirit Redefined." *Progressive Architecture,* Stamford, Connecticut, May 1963, Volume XLIV, Number 5, Pages 200, 204, 207. A review of *Modern Church Architecture.*

Cleve Gray. "Print Review/Pratt Graphic Art Center." *Art in America, New York,* New York, 1963, Volume 51, Number 3, Pages 92-93.

Cleve Gray. "Print Review/Pratt Graphic Art Center." *Art in America,* New York, New York, 1965, Volume 53, Number 2, Pages 112-115.

John Gruen. "Friday Tour of Art." Reviews of New York exhibitions including Albert Christ-Janer's one-man show at Krasner Gallery. *World Journal Tribune,* New York, New York, January 6, 1967, Page 18.

Dorothy Hall. "Three at AAA." *Park East,* New York, New York, January 18, 1973, Page number unknown.

John Davis Hatch, Jr. "New Books on Art." *Magazine of Art,* Toronto, Canada, May, 1940, Volume 33, Number 5, Page 312. A review of *George Caleb Bingham.*

Harold Haydon. "They defy simple categories." *Showcase/Chicago Sun-Times,* Chicago, Illinois, June 17, 1973, Section Three, Page 12.

Donald Hoffman. A review of *George Caleb Bingham. The Kansas City Star,* Kansas City, Missouri, Volume 96, Number 4, September 21, 1975, Section D, Page 1.

Eleanor Jewett. "Renaissance Society's Art Is Satisfying." *Chicago Daily Tribune,* Chicago, Illinois, June 7, 1951, Part 4, Page 5.

Norman Kent. *100 Watercolor Techniques.* Watson-Guptill Publications, New York, New York, 1968, Pages 54-55. An essay entitled "Albert Christ-Janer" with one full-page illustration.

Jim Kinter. "Christ-Janer Art Show Joins Two Worlds." *Daily Intelligencer-Journal,* Lancaster, Pennsylvania, January 12, 1968, Page 11.

Garry Klein. "Tamarind/It's flourishing at UNM, in the opinion of an eminent artist working here now?" *Campus News,* The University of New Mexico, Albuquerque, New Mexico, Volume 7, Number 15, March 2, 1972, Page 3.

Janet Kutner. "The Maturity of Christ-Janer." *The Dallas Morning News,* Dallas, Texas, April 16, 1970, Page 12A.

Janet Kutner. "Diverse art personalities." *The Dallas Morning News,* Dallas, Texas, Volume 125, Number 356, September 21, 1975, Page 38A. A review of *George Caleb Bingham.*

Theodore Law. "Book Reviews." *Magazine of Art,* Toronto, Canada, March, 1947, Volume 40, Number 3, Page 122. A review of *Boardman Robinson.*

Marlan Miller. "New Gallery Brings Distinguished Artist to Valley." *The Phoenix Gazette,* Phoenix, Arizona, Volume 85, Number 43, October 2, 1964, Page 69.

Sybil Moholy-Nagy. "Books." *The Architectural Forum,* New York, New York. January, 1963, Volume 118, Number 1, Page 124. A review of *Modern Church Architecture.*

Paul Pippin. "Reviews/Books." *Progressive Architecture,* Stamford, Connecticut, October, 1948, Volume XXIX, Number 10, Pages 124, 126, 128. A review of *Eliel Saarinen.*

Judith K. Reed. "The Art Book Library/Life of Robinson." *The Art Digest,* Hopewell , New Jersey, October 15, 1946, Volume 21, Number 2, Page 26.

H. R. (Harris Rosenstein?). "Reviews and Previews." *Art News,* New York, New York, February, 1968, Volume 66, Number 10, Page 11. A review of an exhibition at Pratt Institute Gallery.

Nacie Salny. "Happenings in the Arts." *Daily Record,* Morristown,

New Jersey, November 23, 1966, Page 4. A review of Albert Christ-Janer's one-man exhibition at Drew University.

M. S. (Mary Sanders?). "Reviews." *The Architectural Forum,* New York, New York, August, 1948, Volume 89, Number 2, Page 2. A review of *Eliel Saarinen.*

Irving H. Sandler. "Reviews and previews: New Names this month." *Art News,* New York, New York, January, 1963, Volume 61. Number 9, Page 18. A review of an exhibition at Krasner Gallery. *Seaforms* is illustrated.

Archie Satterfield. A review of *George Caleb Bingham. Seattle Post Intelligencer,* Seattle, Washington, Volume 112, Number 229, August 17, 1975, Page G7.

Bernice Schwartz. "Christ-Janer Art Has Movement." *The El Paso Times,* El Paso, Texas, January 22, 1967, Page number unknown.

David L. Shirey. "Reviews and Previews." *Art News,* New York, New York, February, 1973, Volume 72, Number 2, Page 83. *T-72-128* is illustrated on page 82.

Bob Sprague. "Albert Christ-Janer Shows His 'Limitless' Lithographs." *The Bethlehem Globe-Times,* Focus on the Arts, Bethlehem, Pennsylvania, Volume C, Number 32,276, May 8, 1971, Page 9.

Francis J. Quirk. "Special Local Interest in Lehigh Art Show." *The Bethlehem Globe-Times,* Focus on the Arts, Bethlehem, Pennsylvania, Volume C, Number 31,198, November 11, 1967, Page 22.

Harvey Stahl. "In the Galleries." *Arts,* New York, New York, March, 1966, Volume 40, Number 5, Page 59. A review of exhibition at Krasner Gallery.

H. W. Williams, Jr. "Book Review." *College Art Journal,* New York, New York, Autumn, 1947, Volume VII, Number 1, Page 148. A review of *Boardman Robinson.*

UNSIGNED ARTICLES AND CRITIQUES
(Listed chronologically)

"New Art Books." *Art In America,* New York, New York, January, 1940, Volume XXVIII, Number 1, Page 180. A review of *George Caleb Bingham,* 1940.

"Through the River Country." PICTURES/*St. Louis Post Dispatch,* St. Louis, Missouri, October 12, 1941, Page 1.

"The Field of American Art Education/at Michigan State." *The Art Digest,* Hopewell, New Jersey, October 1, 1943, Volume 18, Number 1, Page 25.

"Boardman Robinson/A Review of Albert Christ-Janer's Recent Book." *American Artist,* New York, New York, December, 1946, Volume 10, Number 10, Issue 100, Pages 20-23.

"Christ-Janer Goes to Chicago." *The Art Digest.* Hopewell, New Jersey, September 15, 1947, Volume 21, Number 20, Page 16.

"Required Reading/Behind Saarinen." *Architectural Record,* New York, New York, November, 1948, Volume 104, Number 5, Page 28. A review of *Eliel Saarinen.*

E. B. "Delicacy Is Dominant in Art Exhibited by Albert Christ-Janer." *Chicago Daily Tribune,* Chicago, Illinois, April 28, 1951, Page 12F.

"People in the Arts." *Arts,* New York, New York, March, 1956, Volume 30, Number 6, Page 10.

"People in the Arts." *Arts,* New York, New York, March, 1958, Volume 33, Number 1, Page 12.

"Works of Arthur Davies shown at Lehigh Gallery/Christ-Janer in North Gallery." *The Morning Call,* Allentown, Pennsylvania, Volume 25, Number 139, October 30, 1967, Page 25.

"Exhibit by Christ-Janer To Open in Hop Gallery." *The Dartmouth,* Hanover, New Hampshire, Volume CXXVIII, Number 66, January 24, 1969.

"Two Galleries Set 1-Man Exhibitions." *The Dallas Morning News,* Dallas, Texas, April 5, 1970, Page number unknown.

"Abstractionist to show lithographs at Kemerer Museum." *The Morning Call,* Allentown, Pennsylvania, Volume 26, Number 223, May 6, 1971, Page 64.

"Here Come the Judges." *Orlando Sentinel/Orlando Evening Star,* Orlando, Florida, Volume 87, Number 307, March 16, -972, Page 34-G.

PUBLIC COLLECTIONS
AND EXHIBITIONS

Selected Public Collections

UNITED STATES

The Art Institute of Chicago, Chicago, Illinois
Auburn University, Auburn, Alabama
Museum of Fine Arts, Boston, Massachusetts
The Brooklyn Museum, Brooklyn, New York
Chase Manhattan Bank, New York, New York
Chrysler Museum at Norfolk, Norfolk, Virginia
Cincinnati Art Museum, Cincinnati, Ohio
Concordia College, Moorhead, Minnesota
Coos Art Museum, Coos Bay, Oregon
Cranbrook Academy of Art/Museum, Bloomfield Hills, Michigan
Dartmouth College, Hanover, New Hampshire
El Paso Museum of Art, El Paso, Texas
Franklin and Marshall College, Lancaster, Pennsylvania
Georgia Museum of Art, Athens, Georgia
Gibbes Art Gallery, Charleston, South Carolina
Hamline University Galleries, St. Paul, Minnesota
The High Museum of Art, Atlanta, Georgia
Honolulu Academy of Arts, Honolulu, Hawaii
Honolulu, Hawaii, City and County Collection
Indiana University of Pennsylvania, Indiana, Pennsylvania
Lake Erie College, Painesville, Ohio
Lehigh University Permanent Collections, Bethlehem, Pennsylvania
Loch Haven Art Center, Inc., Orlando, Florida
Malone College, Canton, Ohio
The Metropolitan Museum of Art, New York, New York
Montclair Art Museum, Montclair, New Jersey
Mount Union College, Alliance, Ohio
The Museum of Modern Art, New York, New York
National Air and Space Museum, Washington, D.C.
National Collection of Fine Arts, Washington, D.C.
The New York Public Library, New York, New York

New York University Art Collection, New York, New York
Pennell Collection, Library of Congress, Washington, D.C.
The Pennsylvania Academy of the Fine Arts, Philadelphia, Pennsylvania
The Pennsylvania State University, Museum of Art, University Park, Pennsylvania
Philadelphia Museum of Art, Philadelphia, Pennsylvania
The Phillips Collection, Washington, D.C.
Pratt Institute, New York, New York
Memorial Art Gallery of the University of Rochester, Rochester, New York
The St. Louis Art Museum, St. Louis, Missouri
Saint Olaf College, Northfield, Minnesota
Seattle Art Museum, Seattle, Washington
The Slater Memorial Museum, Norwich, Connecticut
South Bend Museum, South Bend, Indiana
Southern Illinois University, Carbondale, Illinois
St. Joseph's College, West Hartford, Connecticut
Staten Island Institute of Arts and Sciences, Staten Island, New York
State University of New York, New York, New York
Swarthmore College, Swarthmore, Pennsylvania
Syracuse Museum, Syracuse, New York
Texas Fine Arts Association, Austin, Texas
United States Information Agency, Graphic Arts Program, Washington, D.C.
University of Alabama, University, Alabama
University of Illinois, Urbana, Illinois
University of Chicago, Chicago, Illinois
University of Maine, Orono, Maine
Utah State University, Logan, Utah
Walsh College, Canton, Ohio
Wellesley College Museum, Wellesley, Massachusetts
Whitney Museum of American Art, New York, New York
Yale University Art Gallery, New Haven, Connecticut

ABROAD

American Center, U. S. Information Service, Embassy of the United States of America, Stockholm, Sweden

British Museum, London, England

Fitzwilliam Museum, Cambridge, England

Nasjonalgalleriet, Oslo, Norway

Nationalmuseum, Stockholm, Sweden

Norge-Amerika Foreningen, Oslo, Norway

Victoria and Albert Museum, London, England

Exhibitions

1941
November. *Albert Christ-Janer, Russell Green, Gordon Gilkey,* University of Kansas City; traveled to Iowa State Teachers College Art Gallery, Cedar Falls, March 16-28, 1942; Joslyn Art Museum, Omaha, Nebraska; University of Texas, Austin.

1945
November 13—December 16. *Annual Exhibition for Michigan Artists,* Detroit Institute of Arts.

1948
November 4—January 2, 1949. *Fifty-ninth Annual American Exhibition/Water Colors and Drawings,* The Art Institute of Chicago.

1949
May 23—June 23. *Artist Members Exhibition,* The Renaissance Society at the University of Chicago.

1950
April 2-29. *Paintings/Drawings/Sculpture/Prints by Artist Members,* The Renaissance Society at the University of Chicago.

1951
April 15-28. *Christ-Janer,* one-man exhibition, Burton Court Lounge, University of Chicago.

1954
April 9—May 2. *Christ-Janer,* one-man exhibition, C. M. Russell Gallery, Great Falls, Montana.

1955
April 6-24. *Eighty-eighth Annual Exhibition/American Watercolor Society,* American Academy Galleries, New York.

June. *Artist Members Exhibition,* The Renaissance Society at the University of Chicago.

May 4—June 12. *18th Biennial International Water Color Exhibition,* The Brooklyn Museum, Brooklyn, New York.

May 9-15. *Fine Arts Festival* (with John Marin, Adolf Dehn, James Lechay, William Kienbusch, and William Zorach), Saint Olaf College, Northfield, Minnesota; traveled to Charles M. Russell Gallery, Great Falls, Montana, June.

October 7-31. *Albert Christ-Janer, Stuart Frost, and Edwin Zoller,* Ellen Clarke Bertrand Library, Bucknell University, Lewisburg, Pennsylvania.

1956
November 13—December 8. *Arnold Blanch, Adolf Dehn and Albert Christ-Janer,* Saint Paul Gallery, Saint Paul, Minnesota.

December 8-22. *An Exhibition of New Painters at Penn State* (with Stuart Frost, George Pappas, Mary Rubinstein, and Edwin Zoller), The Pennsylvania State University, University Park.

1957
January 13—March 12. *Portrait of Staten Island, 1956,* Staten Island Museum, Staten Island Institute of Arts and Sciences, Staten Island, New York.

January 20—February 24. *The One Hundred and Fifty-Second Annual Exhibition/Water Colors, Prints and Drawings,* The Pennsylvania Academy of the Fine Arts and The Philadelphia Water Color Club, Pennsylvania Academy, Philadelphia.

February 14—March 8. *4 American Artists* (with Arnold Blanch, Adolf Dehn, and Winston McGee), Lake Erie College, Painesville, Ohio.

February 17—March 15. *Contemporary American Watercolors,* The Renaissance Society at the University of Chicago.

1958
March 1-31. *Twenty-one Paintings by Five Members of the Art Faculty,* Pennsylvania State University (with Stuart Frost, George Pappas, Edwin Zoller, and George Zoretich), First Unitarian Church of Pittsburgh.

1959
January 25—March 1. *One Hundred and Fifty-Fourth Annual Exhibition/Water Colors, Prints, Drawings,* The Pennsylvania Academy of the Fine Arts and The Philadelphia Water Color Club, Pennsylvania Academy, Philadelphia.

April 2-19. *The American Watercolor Society/92nd Annual Exhibition,* National Academy Galleries, New York.

September 24—October 9. *Faculty Art Show,* Art School Building, Pennsylvania State University, University Park.

1960
January 10—February 14. *Louis Bouché and Albert Christ-Janer,* Staten Island Museum, Staten Island Institute of Arts and Sciences, Staten Island, New York.

January 26—March 13. *Brooklyn and Long Island Artists,* The Brooklyn Museum, Brooklyn, New York.

February. Group exhibition, Paul Schuster Art Gallery, Cambridge, Massachusetts.

September 10—October 10. *Albert Christ-Janer and Chen Chi,* Sharadin Studio Gallery, Kutztown State College, Kutztown, Pennsylvania; traveled to Swarthmore College, Swarthmore, Pennsylvania, October 3-24; Gettysburg College, Gettysburg, Pennsylvania, November; and Christ-Janer exhibition to Ross Widen Gallery, 11605 Euclid Avenue, Cleveland, Ohio, December 11—January 10, 1961.

1961 May 5—June 4. *47th Annual Exhibition, The Wilmington Society of the Fine Arts,* Delaware Art Center, Wilmington, Delaware. (Christ-Janer was a juror, also, with Carl Zigrosser and Ogden Pleissner.)

1962 February 18—April 15. *Portrait of Staten Island, 1961,* Staten Island Museum, Staten Island Institute of Arts and Sciences, Staten Island, New York.

May 6—June 1. *First Annual College and University Arts Faculty Show,* The Argus Gallery, 2 Green Village Road, Madison, New Jersey.

May 12-13. *Tuxedo Park Art Exhibition and Sale,* The Tuxedo Club, Tuxedo Park, New York.

October 12-14. *The Ninth Annual Brooklyn Heights Art Show,* Grace Church, 254 Hicks Street, Brooklyn, New York. (Christ-Janer was a juror, also, with Edwin Dickinson, Julian Levi, and Maurice Golubov.)

1963 January 7-26. *Christ-Janer,* one-man exhibition, Krasner Gallery, 1061 Madison Avenue, New York.

January 18—March 3. *The One Hundred and Fifty-eighth Annual Exhibition/Water Colors, Prints and Drawings,* The Pennsylvania Academy of the Fine Arts and The Philadelphia Water Color Club, Pennsylvania Academy, Philadelphia.

February 19—April 28. *22nd International Watercolor Biennial,* The Brooklyn Museum, Brooklyn, New York.

March 6—May 26. *Artist Members Exhibition of Murals, Sketches, Drawings, and Water Colors,* The Century Association, 7 West 43rd Street, New York.

May 11-12. *The Second Annual Tuxedo Park Art Exhibition and Sale,* The Tuxedo Club, Tuxedo Park, New York.

June. *Christ-Janer,* one-man exhibition, Saint Olaf College, Northfield, Minnesota.

October 14-31. *Christ-Janer and Chen Chi,* Fine Arts in Jacobson's, 325 North Woodward, Birmingham, Michigan.

1964 April 17-26. *Tenth Annual Brooklyn Heights Art Show,* Plymouth Church, 75 Hicks Street, Brooklyn, New York.

September 20—October 30. *Christ-Janer,* one-man exhibition, Student Center Art Gallery, Seton Hall University, South Orange, New Jersey.

1964 September 27—October. Group exhibition, Gallery of Modern Art, 40 West Main Street, Scottsdale, Arizona.

December 15—January 2, 1965. *Christ-Janer,* one-man exhibition, Krasner Gallery, 1061 Madison Avenue, New York.

1965 January 22—March 7. *The One Hundred and Sixtieth Annual Exhibition/Water Colors, Prints, Drawings,* The Pennsylvania Academy of the Fine Arts and The Philadelphia Water Color Club, Pennsylvania Academy, Philadelphia. (Christ-Janer was a juror, also, with Jimmy Ernst and Benton Spruance.)

April 8-25. *Albert Christ-Janer and Ilse Getz,* Lake Erie College, Painesville, Ohio.

April 23—May 2. *Eleventh Annual Brooklyn Heights Art Show,* Plymouth Church of the Pilgrims, Orange and Hicks Street, Brooklyn, New York.

September 8—October 1. *Christ-Janer,* one-man exhibition, Main Gallery, Pratt Institute, Brooklyn, New York.

December 27—January 9. *Recent Watercolors by Albert Christ-Janer,* The Brooklyn Museum, Brooklyn, New York.

1966 January 4-22. *Christ-Janer,* one-man exhibition, Krasner Gallery, 1061 Madison Avenue, New York.

April 22—May 1. *Twelfth Annual Brooklyn Heights Art Show,* Plymouth Church of the Pilgrims, Orange and Hicks Streets, Brooklyn, New York.

May 1—September 18. *20th National Exhibition of Prints,* Library of Congress, Washington; sponsored by Smithsonian Institution Traveling Exhibition Service, traveled to Albany Institute of History and Art, Albany, New York, October 10-30; College Union, Cornell University, Ithaca, New York, November 5-27; Art Department Eastern Montana College, Billings, Montana, January 14—February 5; George Thomas Hunter Gallery of Art, Chattanooga, Tennessee, February 18—March 12; The Graphic Arts Collection, Princeton University Library, Princeton, New Jersey, April 29—May 21; Norfolk Museum of Arts and Sciences, Norfolk, Virginia, June 3-25; The John & Mable Ringling Museum of Art, Sarasota, Florida, July 2-23; William Rockhill Nelson Gallery of Art, Kansas City, Missouri, August 12—September 3; Colorado Springs Fine Arts Center, Colorado Springs,

Colorado, October 21—November 12; The Taft School, Watertown, Connecticut, March 16—April 7; The Hill School, Pottstown, Pennsylvania, May 1-21.

1966

June 17-26. *Arts and Culture Festival Exhibition of the Prospect Park Centennial,* Prospect Park, Brooklyn, New York.

June 23—July 7. *Christ-Janer,* one-man exhibition, The Whitney Shop, 48 Elm Street, New Canaan, Connecticut.

October 15-28. *Christ-Janer,* one-man exhibition, Hazleton Art League, Inc., 225 East Broad Street, Hazleton, Pennsylvania.

November 9—December 31. *Oil Paintings and Sculpture,* The Century Association, 7 West 43rd Street, New York.

November 18—December 3. *Christ-Janer,* one-man exhibition, Drew University, Madison, New Jersey.

December. *The One Hundred and Sixty-second Annual Exhibition/Prints and Drawings,* The Pennsylvania Academy, of the Fine Arts and The Philadelphia Water Color Club, Pennsylvania Academy, Philadelphia.

1967

January 3-21. *Christ-Janer,* one-man exhibition, Krasner Gallery, 1061 Madison Avenue, New York.

January 19—February 28. *Christ-Janer,* one-man exhibition, El Paso Museum of Art, El Paso, Texas.

February 7-13. *Artists Technical Research Institute Benefit Auction,* Parke-Bernet Galleries, New York.

February 28—March 26. *Christ-Janer/Lithographs/Watercolors,* one-man exhibition, Red River Art Center, 521 Main Street, Moorhead, Minnesota; traveled to Carroll Reece Museum, East Tennessee State University, Johnson City, Tennessee, April 23—July 1.

March. *U. S. Information Agency Traveling Exhibition* to *European Embassies. Landforms 83* received a Purchase Award.

March 18-22. *9th Annual Art Exhibition and Sale,* YM-YWHA, Hillside, New Jersey.

March 31—April 30. *Christ-Janer,* one-man exhibition, Gallery of Modern Art, 40 West Main Street, Scottsdale, Arizona.

April 5—May 27. *Artist Members' Exhibition of Murals, Sketches, Drawings, and Water Colors,* The Century Association, 7 West 43rd Street, New York.

1967

April 21-30. *Thirteenth Annual Brooklyn Heights Art Show,* Plymouth Church of the Pilgrims, 75 Hicks Street, Brooklyn, New York.

June 2-20. *Christ-Janer,* one-man exhibition, Makler Gallery, 1716 Locust Street, Philadelphia.

June 9—August 11. *Invited Exhibition of Water Colors, Prints, and Drawings, The Philadelphia Water Color Club,* The Philadelphia Art Alliance, 251 South 18th Street, Philadelphia.

July. Group exhibition, North Wind Gallery, Charlevoix, Michigan.

October 29—November 21. *Christ-Janer,* one-man exhibition, Alumni Memorial Building Galleries, Lehigh University, Bethlehem, Pennsylvania.

November 14-15. *Albert, Arland, and Victor Christ-Janer,* Arts Festival, Yale University Divinity School (Commons Room Gallery), New Haven, Connecticut.

November 8—December 30. *Oil Paintings and Sculpture,* The Century Association, 7 West 43rd Street, New York.

December 1-18. *Christ-Janer,* one-man exhibition, Wilcox Gallery, Swarthmore College, Swarthmore, Pennsylvania.

December 1-31. *Fiftieth Annual Exhibition, Philadelphia Water Color Club,* The Pennsylvania Academy of the Fine Arts, Philadelphia. *G-4* received M. W. Zimmerman Memorial Prize.

1968

January. Benefit exhibition, Pratt Center for Contemporary Printmaking, Associated American Artists, 605 Fifth Avenue, New York.

January 4-31. *Christ-Janer, Color and Black and White Lithographs,* Institute Gallery, Main Hall, Pratt Institute, Brooklyn, New York.

January 13—February 4. *An Exhibition of Paintings by Albert Christ-Janer,* Goethean Hall Gallery of Art, Franklin and Marshall College, Lancaster, Pennsylvania.

January 18—February 4. *26th Audubon Artists Annual Exhibition,* National Academy Galleries, 1083 Fifth Avenue, New York. (Christ-Janer was a juror, also, for Aquarelle works, with Jack Bookbinder, Alfred D. Crimi, and Avel de Knight.)

January 18—March 3. *American Graphic Workshops: 1968,* The Cincinnati Art Museum, Cincinnati, Ohio. *Landforms 81* received Board of Trustees Purchase Award.

January 19-21. *Fourteenth Annual Brooklyn Heights Art Show*, Plymouth Church of the Pilgrims, 75 Hicks Street, Brooklyn, New York.

February 9-25. *Juried Black and White Exhibition*, The Print Club, 1614 Latimer Street, Philadelphia. *Landforms 82B (Skyforms)* received Mary S. Collins Purchase Prize for the Philadelphia Museum of Art.

February 17—April 14. *29th Annual Exhibition, American Color Print Society*, New Jersey State Museum, Trenton, New Jersey.

February 21—March 17. *39th Northwest Printmakers International Exhibition*, Seattle Art Museum Pavilion; traveled to Portland Art Museum, Portland, Oregon, May 15—June 9.

February 22—March 17. *143rd Annual Exhibition, National Academy of Design*, 1083 Fifth Avenue, New York.

February 27—March 16. *Christ-Janer*, one-man exhibition, Krasner Gallery, 1061 Madison Avenue, New York.

March 11—April 6. *The 49th Annual Exhibition of The Society of American Graphic Artists*, Associated American Artists, 605 Fifth Avenue, New York. *Seaforms 40* received The Addie and Herbert Segerman Purchase Award for the Metropolitan Museum of Art.

April. *12th North Dakota Annual National Print and Drawing Exhibition*, University of North Dakota, Grand Forks.

April 3-27. *1968 Albion College National Print and Drawing Exhibition*, Albion, Michigan.

April 3—May 31. *Artist Members' Exhibition of Murals, Sketches, Drawings, Prints and Water Colors*, The Century Association, 7 West 43rd Street, New York.

April 10—May 10. *Christ-Janer*, one-man exhibition, Studio Gallery, Cypress and Norfolk Avenues, Virginia Beach, Virginia.

April 26-28. *Christ-Janer*, one-man exhibition, State Board of Education Conference, Commonwealth of Virginia, John Marshall Hotel, Richmond, Virginia.

May 29. *Exhibition and Sale, Brooklyn Association for Mental Health Art Exhibit and Sale*, One Grace Court, Brooklyn, New York.

June. *The 49th Annual Exhibition of The Society of American Graphic Artists*, circulated by the Virginia Museum of Fine Arts to colleges, museums and schools in Virginia for two years.

June 10—August 14. *51st Annual Members' Exhibition/ Water Colors, Pastels, Prints, and Drawings, The Philadelphia Water Color Club*, Philadelphia Art Alliance, 251 South 18th Street, Philadelphia.

October 15-19. *Arland and Albert Christ-Janer*, Davis Art Gallery, Stephens College, Columbia, Missouri.

October 29—January 26, 1969. *Sixteenth National Print Exhibition*, The Brooklyn Museum, Brooklyn, New York.

November 13—January 4, 1969. *Autumn Exhibition*, The Century Association, 7 West 43rd Street, New York.

November 23—January 19, 1969. *British International Print Biennale*, Bradford City Art Gallery and Museums, Cartwright Hall, Bradford, England.

December 6-27. *Juried Members' Exhibition*, The Print Club, 1614 Latimer Street, Philadelphia. *Skyforms 85* received Lessing J. Rosenwald Purchase Prize for the Philadelphia Museum of Art.

December 12-29. *Annual Print and Drawing Exhibition*, The National Arts Club, 15 Gramercy Park, New York. *Skyforms 78B* (erroneously listed as *Seaforms 42*) received National Arts Club Bronze Medal.

January 1-31. *Christ-Janer*, one-man exhibition, University of Maine, Orono.

January 17-March 2. *The One Hundred and Sixty-fourth Annual Exhibition*, The Pennsylvania Academy of the Fine Arts and The Philadelphia Water Color Club, Pennsylvania Academy, Philadelphia.

January 23—February 23. *Christ-Janer*, one-man exhibition, Beaumont-May Gallery, Hopkins Center, Dartmouth College, Hanover, New Hampshire.

February 6—March 9. *40th Northwest Printmakers International Exhibition*, Seattle Art Museum Pavilion, Seattle, Washington; traveled to Portland, Oregon, April 11-27. *Seaforms 74B* received Honorable Mention and was purchased by Seattle Museum.

February 7-27. *Juried Black and White Print Exhibit*, The Print Club, 1614 Latimer Street, Philadelphia. *Seaforms 50A (Oriental Landscape)* received The William H. Walker Prize for the Philadelphia Museum of Art.

February 23—March 9. *29th Members' Exhibition, Art Directors Club*, New York.

1969

February 27—March 23. *144th Annual Exhibition, National Academy of Design,* 1083 Fifth Avenue, New York. Watercolor Section. Purchased for the Henry Ward Ranger Fund, assigned to Tacoma Art Museum, Tacoma, Washington.

March 4-30. *The Boston Printmakers 21st Annual Exhibition,* Museum of Fine Arts, Boston.

March 7-28. *Ninth Annual Print Exhibition,* State University of New York College, Potsdam.

March 30—May 10. *Thirteenth National Print Exhibition,* Hunterdon Art Center, Old Stone Mill, Center Street, Clinton, New Jersey; traveled to Public Library of Newark, June; Cultural Center of Ocean City, July.

April 8-26. *Painters and Sculptors Society of New Jersey, 28th Annual National Exhibition,* Jersey City Museum, Jersey City Main Library, 472 Jersey Avenue, Jersey City, New Jersey.

April 15-30. *Festival of the Arts,* New York City Community College, Brooklyn, New York.

April 25—May 9. *Fifth Annual A.A.C. National Print Competition,* Auburn University, Auburn, Alabama. *Seaforms 41* received Purchase Award.

April 30—May 31. *Artist Members' Exhibition of Murals, Sketches, Drawings, Prints and Water Colors,* The Century Association, 7 West 43rd Street, New York.

May 1-30. *Graphics '69, National Print and Drawing Exhibition,* The Francis McCray Gallery, Western New Mexico University, Silver City.

May 5-30. *The 50th Annual Exhibition of The Society of American Graphic Artists,* Associated American Artists, 663 Fifth Avenue, New York. *Landforms 63* was included in a traveling exhibition selected from *The 50th Annual Exhibition* for a tour of the Near East, circulated by United States Information Agency.

June 4—August 8. *52nd Annual Members' Exhibition, The Philadelphia Water Color Club,* Philadelphia Art Alliance, 251 South 18th Street, Philadelphia. *Number 13* was included in a traveling exhibition to Wilson College, Chambersburg, Pennsylvania, September; Juniata College, Huntingdon, Pennsylvania, November 28—December 19; Bucknell University, Lewisburg, Pennsylvania, January, 1970; Lycoming College, Williamsport, Pennsylvania, April, 1970.

1969

July 21-31. *Christ-Janer,* one-man exhibition, Munson Gallery, Old South Wharf, Nantucket, Massachusetts.

September 22—October 10. *Original Prints from the Pratt Graphic Arts Center,* Pratt Institute Art Gallery, Brooklyn, New York.

October 6-10. *Christ-Janer,* one-man exhibition, College Center, Southern State College, Magnolia, Arkansas.

Ocober 12-30. *The National Arts Club 71st Annual Watercolor Exhibition,* The National Arts Club, 15 Gramercy Park, New York. (Christ-Janer was a juror, also, with Chen Chi, Ranulph Bye, Edwin Dahlbert, and Dale Meyers.)

November 2-23. *Colorprint U.S.A.,* Texas Tech University, Lubbock.

November 12—January 4. *Autumn Exhibition,* The Century Association, 7 West 43rd Street, New York.

December 6-10. *15th Annual American Art at Mid-Century Exhibition and Sale,* YM-YWHA, 760 Northfield Avenue, West Orange, New Jersey.

1970

January 5-10. *Pratt Graphics Center Benefit Exhibition,* Associated American Artists, 663 Fifth Avenue, New York.

January 8-30. *Christ-Janer,* one-man exhibition, Loenig Art Gallery, Concordia Teachers College, Seward, Nebraska; traveled to Gallery of Modern Art, 40 West Main Street, Scottsdale, Arizona, February 15—March 15; Cushing Galleries, 2800 Routh Street, Dallas, Texas, April 1-30; B. K. Smith Gallery, Lake Erie College, Painesville, Ohio, May 10—June 10; The Paine Art Center and Arboretum, Oshkosh, Wisconsin, August 30—September 30.

January 12-30. *Christ-Janer,* one-man exhibition, Associated American Artists, 663 Fifth Avenue, New York.

January 22—February 8. *28th Audubon Artists Annual Exhibition,* National Academy Galleries, New York.

January 29—February 27. *A Selection of Contemporary American Prints,* State University of New York, Oneonta.

February 1-15. *30th Members' Exhibition,* Art Directors Club, Lever Brothers Company Auditorium, 390 Park Avenue, New York. *Skyforms 57B* received First Prize in Graphics.

April 3-30. *Georgia State University—Oxford First Annual National Print Exhibition,* University Gallery, Georgia State University, Atlanta; traveled to Valdosta (Georgia) State College, University of South Florida, Florida Presby-

113

terian College, Virginia Commonwealth University, and Illinois Institute of Technology, through March, 1971.

1970

April 1—May 15. *Christ-Janer,* one-man exhibition, Southeastern Community College, Whiteville, North Carolina.

April 5—May 15. *Fourteenth National Print Exhibition,* Hunterdon Art Center, Old Stone Mill, Clinton, New Jersey; traveled to Bergen Community Museum, Paramus, New Jersey, June; Morris Museum of Arts and Sciences, Morristown, New Jersey, July and August.

April 7-25. *29th Annual National Exhibition, Painters and Sculptors Society of New Jersey,* Jersey City Museum.

April 7-25. *National Print Exhibition/39th Festival of the Arts,* State University of New York, Potsdam.

April 8—May 17. *Work on Paper,* The Century Association, 7 West 43rd Street, New York.

April 19—May 6. *The Boston Printmakers 22nd Annual Exhibition,* Copley Society, 158 Newbury Street, Boston, Massachusetts; traveled to Goldfarb Library, Brandeis University, Waltham, Massachusetts, May 10-31.

May 9—June 7. *53rd Annual Members' Exhibition, The Philadelphia Water Color Club,* Museum of The Philadelphia Civic Center, 34th Street at Civic Center Boulevard, Philadelphia. *Skyforms 77* selected for traveling exhibition, 1970-71.

May 9—June 28. *Sixth National Print and Drawing Competition,* Dulin Gallery of Art, Knoxville, Tennessee.

July 15—September 13. *Watermedia Painting Exhibition,* Gallery of Art, Henderson Museum, University of Colorado, Boulder.

September—November. *Second British International Print Biennale,* Bradford City Art Gallery and Museum, Cartwright Hall, Bradford, England.

October. *Lawton-Fort Sill Art Council Exhibition,* Museum of the Great Plains, Lawton, Oklahoma. *Seaforms 47* received Purchase Award.

October 25—November 29. *Sixth Annual Piedmont Graphics Exhibition,* The Mint Museum of Art, Charlotte, North Carolina. *Seaforms 75B* received Honorable Mention.

December 6—January 2, 1971. *Prints 1970-1971,* Cheltenham Art Center, 439 Ashbourne Road, Cheltenham, Pennsylvania.

1971

January 24-30. *Gardens Art Festival Eight,* Holiday Inn of Callaway Gardens, Pine Mountain, Georgia.

February 1-28. *First Annual New Mexico Art League National Small Painting Exhibition,* University of New Mexico, Albuquerque. *Seaforms W121* received Purchase Award.

February 4—March 7. *1st Hawaii National Print Exhibition,* Honolulu Academy of Arts, Honolulu.

February 7-25. *Christ-Janer,* one-man exhibition, Visual Arts Building Foyer, The University of Georgia, Athens.

February 21—March 13. *3rd National Printing Show/Fine Arts Festival,* Washington and Jefferson College, Washington, Pennsylvania.

March 1-31. *The 3rd Biennial Exhibition of Prints and Drawings,* Dickinson State College, Dickinson, North Dakota.

March 7-31. *Graphics '71, Second Biennial National Print and Drawing Exhibition,* The Francis McCray Gallery, Western New Mexico University, Silver City.

March 9-25. *Lawton Junior Service League/Second Annual Juried Exhibition/Painting and Sculpture,* Museum of the Great Plains, Lawton, Oklahoma.

April. *Colorprint, U.S.A.,* Texas Tech University, Lubbock.

April. *7th National Print Exhibition,* Springfield College, Springfield, Massachusetts. *Skyforms 72* received Purchase Award.

April 10—May 17. *35th National Graphic Arts and Drawing Exhibition,* Wichita Art Association, 9112 East Central, Wichita, Kansas.

April 13—May 1. *30th Annual National Exhibition 1971, Painters and Sculptors Society of New Jersey,* Jersey City Museum. *Skyforms 98* received Sebastian Bienfang Prize.

May 1—June 15. *Sixtieth Annual Exhibition, Texas Fine Arts Association,* Austin.

May 2-23. *7th National Print Exhibition,* Springfield College, Springfield, Massachusetts.

May 2-30. *13th Annual National Exhibition of Prints and Drawings,* Oklahoma Art Center, Oklahoma City.

May 2-30. *Sixth Annual Central South Exhibition,* The Tennessee Art League and The Parthenon of Nashville, Nashville, Tennessee.

May 7—June 20. *Seventh Dulin National Print and Drawing Competition,* The Dulin Gallery of Art, Knoxville, Tennessee.

May 9-28. *Christ-Janer,* one-man exhibition, Annie S. Kemerer Museum, Bethlehem, Pennsylvania.

June 6-30. *Graphics, U.S.A.,* Robert Paul Gallery, 67 East Oak, Chicago, Illinois.

June 13—August 21. *2nd Annual Watercolor West,* University Gallery, Utah State University, Logan.

July 4-25. *14th National Jury Show,* Chautauqua Exhibition of American Art, Chautauqua, New York.

July 15—September 13. *Watermedia Painting,* Henderson Museum Gallery of Art, University of Colorado, Boulder.

July 26-30. *International Platform Association Exhibition,* Cleveland Heights, Ohio.

July 31—September 5. *61st Annual Exhibition, Connecticut Academy of Fine Arts,* Wadsworth Atheneum, Hartford.

August. *18th Annual Exhibition of Contemporary American Paintings,* Lehigh University, Bethlehem, Pennsylvania. *Skyforms W 128* received Purchase Award.

August. *United States Information Agency Exhibition,* Philadelphia Art Alliance, 251 South 18th Street, Philadelphia. *Skyforms 58A* selected for USIA traveling exhibition in Europe.

August 23—October 22. *Christ-Janer,* one-man exhibition, Provident National Bank, Broad and Chestnut Streets, Philadelphia.

September 8-22. *The 51st Exhibition of The Society of American Graphic Artists,* Kennedy Galleries, 20 East 56th Street, New York.

September 8-24. *32nd Annual Exhibition, American Color Print Society,* Philadelphia Art Alliance, 251 South 18th Street, Philadelphia.

October 4-31. *Christ-Janer,* one-man exhibition, Hetzel Union Gallery, The Pennsylvania State University, University Park.

October 22-25. *1971 International Art Show, Lawton-Fort Sill Art Council,* Lawton, Oklahoma.

November 7—December 5. *Georgia Artists,* The High Museum of Art, Atlanta.

November 14—December 17. *Art on Paper,* The Dillard Paper Company and The Weatherspoon Guild, The Weatherspoon Art Gallery; The University of North Carolina, Greensboro.

November 21—December 19. *Juried Exhibition of Prints and Photography,* Cheltenham Arts Centre, Cheltenham, Pennsylvania.

November 21—December 30. *Eighth Annual Piedmont Graphics Exhibition,* The Mint Museum of Art, Charlotte, North Carolina.

December 5—January 4, 1972. *4th Annual National Print Exhibition,* San Diego State College, San Diego, California.

December 5—January 16, 1972. *Lauren Rogers Regional Exhibition,* Laurel, Mississippi.

December 6-29. *Man and the Environment, Third National Invitational Exhibition/Printmaking,* The University of Wisconsin, Green Bay.

January. *Audubon Artists Annual Exhibition,* National Academy Galleries, 1083 Fifth Avenue, New York.

February 21—March 17. *Third Annual Exhibition of Paintings and Sculpture,* Lawton-Fort Sill Art Council, Museum of the Great Plains, Lawton, Oklahoma.

February 26—March 17. *55th Annual Members' Exhibition, The Philadelphia Water Color Club,* Capuzzi Studio, Philadelphia.

February 29—March 17. *Watercolor Invitational Exhibition,* Chico State College, Chico, California.

March 11—April 5. *Christ-Janer,* one-man exhibition, Cushing Galleries, 2723 Fairmont, Dallas, Texas.

March 19—April 29. *Davidson National Print and Drawing Competition,* Stowe Gallery, Davidson College, Davidson, North Carolina.

April 7-30. *36th Semi-annual Southeastern Exhibit,* Gallery of Contemporary Art, Winston-Salem, North Carolina.

April 9-26. *15th Annual North Dakota Print and Drawing Exhibition,* University of North Dakota, Grand Forks.

April 9-26. *Colorprint U.S.A.,* Texas Tech University, Lubbock.

April 22—May 19. *9th National Monroe Annual,* Masur Museum of Art, Monroe, Louisiana.

April 30—May. *14th National Print and Drawing Exhibition, Oklahoma Art Center,* Oklahoma City.

1972

April 30—May 28. *Seventh Annual Central South Exhibition,* The Tennessee Art League and The Parthenon of Nashville, Nashville, Tennessee.

May 6—June 4. *61st Annual Exhibition, Texas Fine Arts Association,* Austin.

May 7-21. *15th National Exhibition, Greater Fall River Art* Association, Fall River, Massachusetts.

May 7-28. *8th National Print Exhibition,* Springfield College, Springfield, Massachusetts.

June. *Georgia Artists Exhibition,* Museum of Arts and Sciences, Macon.

July 1-30. *The Art Association of Newport, Sixty-first Annual Exhibition,* 78 Bellevue Avenue, Newport, Rhode Island.

August 29—September 27. *Christ-Janer,* one-man exhibition, Fine Arts Gallery, University of Colorado, Boulder.

September. *Opening Exhibition,* The Frankenberg-Guthrie Gallery, 95 Hoyt Street, Athens, Georgia.

September 9—October 8. *62nd Annual Exhibition, Connecticut Academy of Fine Arts,* Wadsworth Atheneum, Hartford.

October. *Colorprint U.S.A.,* Texas Tech University, Lubbock.

October. *Christ-Janer,* one-man exhibition, The Flaten Gallery, Saint Olaf College, Northfield, Minnesota.

October 29—November 13. *50th Regional Exhibition, Shreveport Art Guild,* 1032 Ontario, Shreveport, Louisiana.

November 12-26. *Albert Christ-Janer/Watercolors and Prints,* Loch Haven Art Center, Orlando, Florida; traveled to Gibbes Art Gallery, Charleston, South Carolina, December 15—January 7, 1973.

November 12—December 10. *Georgia Artists 2,* The High Museum of Art, Atlanta.

November 12—December 19. *Art on Paper,* Dillard Paper Company and the Weatherspoon Guild, Weatherspoon Art Gallery; The University of North Carolina, Greensboro, North Carolina.

November 26—December 31. *Ninth Annual Piedmont Graphics Exhibition,* The Mint Museum of Art, Charlotte, North Carolina. *Sandia Crest 101* received Honorable Mention.

December 3-31. *17th National Sun Carnival,* El Paso Museum of Art, El Paso, Texas. *Seaforms G5* received Purchase Award.

1973

January. *Christ-Janer,* one-man exhibition, Georgia Center for Continuing Education, The University of Georgia, Athens.

January 13-19. *Gardens Art Festival Ten,* Holiday Inn of Callaway Gardens, Pine Mountain, Georgia. *Sandia Crest 103* received Honorable Mention.

January 3—February 1. *Christ-Janer,* one-man exhibition, Intown Club, 1375 Euclid Avenue, Cleveland, Ohio.

January 7-28. *Invitational Print Exhibition,* University of Alabama, University, Alabama.

January 8-27. *Results of Tamarind,* one-man exhibition, Associated American Artists, 663 Fifth Avenue, New York.

January 18-31. *Christ-Janer,* one-man exhibition, Heath Gallery, 34 Lombardy Way, N.E., Atlanta, Georgia.

January 21—February 17. *Christ-Janer,* one-man exhibition, Discovery Art Galleries, 1191 Valley Road, Clifton, New Jersey.

February. *Christ-Janer,* one-man exhibition, South Arkansas Arts Center, El Dorado.

February 10—March 11. *1st Annual Images on Paper,* Springfield Art Association, 700 North Fourth Street, Springfield, Illinois. *Seaforms GA 12* received a Purchase Award.

March—April. *Contemporary Watercolor Exhibition* (with Chen Chi, Gladys Nilsson, William Wiley, Paul Jenkins, Robert Natkin), Western Illinois University, Macomb.

March 6—April 1. *14th Dixie Annual,* Montgomery Museum of Fine Arts, Montgomery, Alabama.

March 12—April 7. *The 52nd Annual Exhibition of The Society of American Graphic Artists,* Associated American Artists, 663 Fifth Avenue, New York; traveled to Van Straaten Gallery, 646 North Michigan Avenue, Chicago, Illinois, May 15—June 15.

March 15—April 15. *4th Biennial International Matmedia Exhibition,* Dickinson State College, Dickinson, North Dakota.

March 15—May 15. *Christ-Janer,* one-man exhibition, First National Bank, 101 Lumpkin Street, Athens, Georgia.

March 18—April 6. *Graphics '73, Third Biennial National Print and Drawing Exhibition,* The Francis McCray Gallery, Western New Mexico University, Silver City.

March 18—May 20. *The Boston Printmakers 25th Anniversary Exhibition*, De Cordova Museum, Lincoln, Massachusetts.

March 20—April 5. *The William McKinley Visiting Scholar Program* (lecture and exhibition), Malone College, Canton, Ohio, March 20-23; Walsh College, Canton, Ohio, March 26-29; Mount Union College, Alliance, Ohio, April 2-5.

April. *Exhibition of Prints and Drawings*, Oklahoma Art Association, Oklahoma City. *Seaforms GA 12* received Purchase Award.

April—May. *Sixty-second Annual Exhibition, Texas Fine Arts Association*, Austin. *Seaforms D 24* received the Mr. and Mrs. Frank A. Gibson Purchase Prize.

April 13—May 9. *Open Juried Exhibition*, The Print Club, 1614 Latimer Street, Philadelphia, Pennsylvania.

April 20—May 13. *1st Miami Graphics Biennial*, Miami Art Center, Miami, Florida.

April 27—May 27. *2nd Hawaii National Print Exhibition*, Honolulu Academy of Arts, Honolulu. *Moonforms GA 17* received Purchase Award.

April 29—May 27. *Eighth Annual Central South Art Exhibition*, The Tennessee Art League and The Parthenon of Nashville, Nashville, Tennessee.

April 30—May 4. *Fourth Annual National Print Exhibition*, The First National Bank of Atlanta and Georgia State University, First National Bank Tower Lobby; traveled to Georgia State University Gallery, May 11-25; Wesleyan College, Macon, Georgia, October 8-26; University of South Carolina, Columbia, South Carolina, November 5-16; Columbus Museum of Arts & Crafts, Columbus, Georgia, January 3-31, 1974.

May 6—June 6. *15th Annual National Print and Drawing Exhibition*, Oklahoma Art Center, Oklahoma City. *Moonforms GA 14* received Juror's Recommended Purchase Award.

May 8-22. *1973 National Print Exhibition*, Western Illinois University, Macomb.

May 30—June 24. *New Watercolors and Tamarind Lithographs by Albert Christ-Janer*, The Midway Studio Galleries, University of Chicago.

June 1—July 1. *Three Contemporary Printmakers/Albert Christ-Janer, Jacob Kainen and Tadeusz Lapinski*, National Collection of Fine Arts, Washington, D. C.

June 14—July 22. *56th Annual Exhibition, Philadelphia Water Color Club*, Philadelphia. *Sandia Crest 105* received The Alice McFadden Eyre Medal.

June 25—July 20. *National Exhibition of Works on Paper '73*, Georgia Association for the Advancement of Art, Atlanta.

June. *Albert Christ-Janer, Charles Massey, and Grant Tittle*, Art Dimensions, 808 Montana, El Paso, Texas.

July 1-29. *63rd Annual Exhibition, Connecticut Academy of Fine Arts*, Wadsworth Atheneum, Hartford. *Seaforms GA 12* received Barbara Padorowsky Memorial Prize.

August 15—September 9. *1st National Print Exhibition*, Los Angeles Printmaking Society, North Hollywood, California. *Sandia Crest 106* received Purchase Award.

September 21—November 25. *23rd National Exhibition of Prints*, Library of Congress and National Collection of Fine Arts, exhibited at National Collection, Washington, D. C., and circulated in the United States.

October. *1st New Hampshire Graphics Annual*, Nashua.

October. *Invitational Exhibition*, Cumberland College, Williamsburg, Kentucky.

October 24—November 11. *Christ-Janer*, Oslo Foreningen, Radhusgt 19, Oslo, Norway.

November 4-19. *51st Regional Art Exhibition, Shreveport Art Club and Shreveport Art Guild*, Shreveport, Louisiana. *Seaforms D 37* received Purchase Prize.

November 4-20. *Watercolor 33*, Birmingham Museum of Art, Birmingham, Alabama.

November 11—December 9. *Printmaking Now*, West Texas Museum, Lubbock. *Moonforms GA 16* received Purchase Award.

November 14-30. *Christ-Janer*, one-man exhibition, American Center, American Embassy, Sveavagen, Stockholm, Sweden.

November 14—January 6, 1974. *California College of Arts and Crafts World Print Competition*, San Francisco Museum of Art, San Francisco.

December 2—January 6, 1974. *Tenth Annual Piedmont Graphics Exhibition*, The Mint Museum of Art, Charlotte, North Carolina. *Moonforms 18* received Purchase Award.

December 14—January 11, 1974. *Juried Members' Exhibition,* The Print Club, 1614 Latimer Street, Philadelphia.

January 7-28. *Invitational Print Exhibition,* University of Alabama, University, Alabama.

January 18—February 11. *Albert Christ-Janer and Ray K. Metzker,* The Print Club, 1614 Latimer Street, Philadelphia.

February 24—March 18. *Members' Exhibition, Alabama Water Color Society,* Birmingham Museum of Art, Birmingham, Alabama.

February. *Christ-Janer,* one-man exhibition, Venable/Neslage Galleries, 1625 Connecticut Avenue, N.W., Washington, D.C.

March 6—April 13. *Christ-Janer,* one-man exhibition, The Frankenburg-Guthrie Gallery, 95 Hoyt Street, Athens, Georgia.

April 1-30. *Albert Christ-Janer,* one-man exhibition, Lake Erie College, Painesville, Ohio.

May 4—June 9. *Sixty-third Annual Exhibition,* Texas Fine Arts Association, Austin. *Skyforms D 25* received Halton Purchase Prize.

May. Group exhibition, The Frankenburg-Guthrie Gallery, 95 Hoyt Street, Athens, Georgia.

May 28—June 14. *A Tribute Exhibition: Albert W. Christ-Janer, Prints and Paintings,* Pratt Institute, Brooklyn, New York. (Exhibition coincided with commencement and the posthumous award of an Honorary Citation.)

August 22, 1974—April 10, 1975. *Texas Fine Arts Association Traveling Exhibitions D and F,* circulated in Texas: *D* to Crane, Slaton, Plainview, Pampa, Clarendon, Amarillo, Snyder, Levelland, Lubbock; *F* to McKinney, Sherman, Clarksville, Mesquite, Sweetwater, Grand Prairie, Waco, Ingram.

November 3-23. *Second New Hampshire International Graphics Annual,* Nashua Arts and Science Center, Nashua, New Hampshire; traveled to New London and Plymouth, New Hampshire; San Francisco, California; Woodstock, Ontario; Scottsbluff, Nebraska.

December 3-31. *Albert Christ-Janer, Prints and Paintings.* Centennial Year Celebration, Saint Olaf College, Northfield, Minnesota.

March 26—April 10. *Graphics Exhibition,* The National Arts Club, 15 Gramercy Park, New York. *Sandia Crest 101* received Honorable Mention.

April 26—May 25. *2nd Miami Graphics Biennial,* Miami Art Center, Miami, Florida.

May 4-31. *Ninth Dulin National Print and Drawing Competition,* The Dulin Gallery of Art, Knoxville, Tennessee.

May. *Sixty-fourth Annual Exhibition,* Texas Fine Arts Association, Austin, Texas.

October 10—November 9. *3rd Hawaii National Print Exhibition,* Honolulu Academy of Arts, Honolulu.

Credits

Henry J. Hulett, catalogue #2, 16, 20, 21, 22, 25, 37, 42, 60, 63

W. Robert Nix and Wiley Sanderson, catalogue #18, 28, 29, 30, 31, 32, 52, 53, 64, 75, 95, 97, 98, 102, 108

William G. Murray, catalogue #69, 70, 71, 84, 87, 88, 99, 103, 105, 109, 110, 113, 114, 115

The Brooklyn Museum, catalogue #17

Memorial Art Museum of the University of Rochester, catalogue #19

Whitney Museum of American Art, catalogue #27

Dartmouth College, catalogue #36

Kay Studio, p. 82 (top)

Paul Parsons, p. 82 (bottom)

Courtesy of The Pennsylvania State University, p. 85 (bottom)

Courtesy Pratt Institute, p. 86, 87 (top)

Jules Schick, p. 88

Courtesy Tamarind Institute, The University of New Mexico, p. 91 (left)

Mary Hammond, p. 91 (right)

Birkhaug & Omdal, p. 92 (lower left)

2,500 copies of this catalogue were printed by
The University of Georgia Printing Department.

Edited by Ethel Moore
Designed by Martyn Hitchcock

Text is set in 10 on 13 pt. Times Roman Type
Color reproduction by Lithoplates, Atlanta, Ga.
Text paper is 80 lb. Beckett Brilliant Opaque, Satin finish
Cover stock is 10 pt. Kromekote slate